Discovering American Culture

2nd Edition

Cheryl L. Delk

Georgia State University

Ann Arbor
University of Michigan Press

Acknowledgments

I am very grateful for having been given the opportunity to improve one of the first projects of my professional career in ESL. I will always be thankful to my first mentor in the field, Amy Tickle, and other friends and former colleagues in Michigan who supported me with the original project as well as my current colleagues in Georgia whose patience during this revision was also greatly appreciated.

Grateful acknowledgement is given to the following authors, publishers, and individuals for permission to reprint their materials or previously published materials.

American Baby for Cris Beam, "The Changing American Family," *American Baby,* May 2005.

Houghton-Mifflin Company for excerpt of page from *The American Heritage Dictionary of the English Language, Fourth Edition.* Copyright © 2006. Reprinted by permission.

The following sources are also acknowledged:

Ben Colman for photo page 69.

The Detroit News for "Making Teamwork Work," 1994.

Gannett News Service for "Actions Speak Louder than Words" and "Silent Messages," 1993.

Georgia State University for Fall 2007 Recreation Rap-Up website.

iStockphoto.com

Margareta Larsson, Lauren Naimola, and John Stowe for photos page 129.

National Textbook Company, "The Analysis of Familiar Cultures" from *The Cultural Revolution in Foreign Language Teaching,* ed. Robert C. Lafayette, 1975.

The New York Times Almanac, 2007, edited by John W. Wright. New York: Penguin Group, 2007.

Oxford University Press for the activity adapted from Barry Tomalin and Susan Stempleski, *Cultural Awareness* (Hong Kong: Oxford University Press, 1993): 65–68.

Parks & Recreation by Daniel Atilano, "Tracking the Trends, *Parks & Recreation,* 41, no. 3 (March 2006).

Population Bulletin for lecture on older generation, from page 4, volume 55, December 2000.

U.S. Department of Education, National Center for Education Statistics "National Public Education Financial Survey 2002–03"; June 2006 and September 2006 statistics.

www.collegeboard.com

For voice talent: Lindsay Devine, Pat Grimes, Stephanie Grohoski, Scott Ham, Badria Jazairi, Lindsay Sarin, and Jeremy Sobczak.

Every effort has been made to contact the copyright holders for permission to reprint borrowed material. We regret any oversights that may have occurred and will rectify them in future printings of this book.

Contents

To the Teacher   vii

To the Student   viii

1. Taking Off: A First Look at Culture   1
Vocabulary Development   3
I.   Who Studies Culture?   4
II.   Different Views of Learning Culture   7
III. Generalizations and Stereotypes   8
IV.   How to Talk about Culture   14
V.   Values Application   18

2. Speaking Out: How Americans Communicate   27
Vocabulary Development   29
I.   Introductions and Other Encounters   30
II.   American Conversation   35
III. Nonverbal Communication   40
IV.   Values Application   50

3. Working Out: Sports and Fitness in the United States   51
Vocabulary Development   54
I.   Popular Sports in the United States   57
II.   History of Extreme Sports   67
III. Americans and Fitness   70
IV.   Values Application   74

4. Hitting the Books: The American Education System   75
Vocabulary Development   78
I.   Philosophy of American Education   81
II.   The Organization of American Schools   83
III. Enrollment in American Schools   91
IV.   American Higher Education   94
V.   Problems in American Education   101
VI.   Values Application   105

5. Earning a Living: The American Workplace   107

   Vocabulary Development   110

   I.   Different Types of Occupations in the United States   111

   II.   Earnings and Benefits   119

   III. How Americans Work   124

   IV.   Values Application   128

6. Getting Along: Family Life in the United States   129

   Vocabulary Development   131

   I.   Traditional Family Structures   132

   II.   Changing Family Structures   134

   III. The Older Generation   146

   IV.   American Homes   148

   V.   Values Application   149

   Appendix: Vocabulary from the Academic Word List Appearing in This Text   151

To the Teacher

Format of the Textbook

Each chapter in *Discovering American Culture* follows a similar format, divided into these sections.

Opening Activity: Each chapter opens with an activity that will help students to preview or think about the topic of the chapter. This opening activity may be as simple as a photo or may involve a detailed activity. Its purpose is to raise the students' awareness of the topic.

Each chapter contains a brief review of the previous chapter and an overview of what the students will study in the current chapter. In addition, each chapter lists the language objectives; instructors are encouraged to review these with the students before studying the chapter as a preview. Teachers are encouraged to use the book in chronological order.

Vocabulary Development: All chapters include a section on vocabulary development so that the students either have lists of important words and/or learn strategies for developing their vocabularies.

Content Heading: Each chapter is divided into content areas marked with roman numerals. With each content area, activities (labeled A, B, C, etc.) help students comprehend the material through integrated language skills activities.

Values Application: After an introduction to cultural values in Chapter 1, each subsequent chapter has a final section called Values Application that gives students the opportunity to reflect on shared cultural values among Americans.

Listening: Activities that make use of the audio are preceded by ⓔ. Scripts can be found in the Instructor's Notes available at **www.press.umich.edu/esl/**. Of course, teachers always have the option of reading from the scripts.

The content material is supplemented with activities that assist students in comprehension. The material has been carefully chosen and analyzed to determine those language skills that will best assist students in comprehending the information provided.

New in the Second Edition

- updated readings and updated visual and content information
- a new chapter on sports and fitness in the United States
- additional writing activities
- additional academic strategies highlighted in language boxes
- language objectives provided in the student textbook
- additional information and activities for instructors on the Internet
- words from the Academic Word List in readings and activities listed in the Appendix

To the Student

Learning to understand a culture very different from our own is a difficult task. As you continue studying English, you will see that language and culture are closely linked. This book will help you learn about another culture and then introduce you to aspects of the culture that many Americans share.

Activities in this book will help you:

- understand American culture in terms of values, behavior, beliefs
- identify some dominant American values and their role in American society
- comprehend different aspects of the patterns of living among many Americans

Each chapter and activity has been designed to help you improve your English skills. There is a focus in this book on improving your listening and reading comprehension as well as your ability to speak and write in English.

Chapter 1 provides an introduction to the study of culture, which includes some terms used in the field of anthropology, as well as a review of cultural values that are sometimes used to make cross-cultural comparisons. You will learn strategies to express your opinions and be introduced to some basic values that are used to compare cultures. The other chapters cover different aspects of culture: communication, sports & fitness, education, working, and the family. You will be given several opportunities to express your opinions on cross-cultural issues.

CHAPTER 1

Taking Off:
A First Look at Culture

Read the items listed. Which of these words do you associate with the word *culture?*

art	family	communication	music
money	politics	education	food
television	sports	history	literature
movies	gestures	holidays	proverbs/idioms
houses	cooking	language	clothing

This chapter looks at the connection between anthropology and culture and discusses what culture means in terms of the beliefs, behavior, and values of a society. You will learn how to avoid stereotypes as you learn to distinguish various cultural values. You will practice language skills including:

- skimming a text for the main idea
- classifying information from a text into a graphic organizer
- listening for specific words
- using qualifiers and distinguishing between *too* and *very*
- making comparisons
- expressing opinion; agreeing and disagreeing
- identifying different word forms
- scanning a text for specific information
- finding definitions in a text

After completing this chapter, return to this page and assess how well you did in reaching these objectives.

Vocabulary Development

This list contains some words from this chapter that may be new to you. Review the list, and put a check (✔) next to the words you recognize and feel comfortable using. When you are finished with the chapter, return to this list and make sure you can put a check next to all of the words.

anthropology ____	ethnography ____	complex ____
outgoing ____	ethnic ____	diversity ____
linguistics ____	ancestor ____	archaeology ____
transform ____	evolve ____	judgment ____
context ____	participant ____	observer ____
custom ____	aggressive ____	dialect ____
individualism ____	cooperation ____	informality ____
cooperation ____	formality ____	equality ____
tradition ____	competition ____	materialism ____
practicality ____	progress ____	privacy ____
directness ____	analyze ____	cultural ____
evolve ____	institution ____	similar ____
distinctive ____	emphasize ____	focus ____
research ____	contribute ____	dominate ____
factor ____	evaluate ____	affect ____

I. Who Studies Culture?

A. Skim the reading on page 5. What do you think it will be about?

> **Skimming**
>
> Skimming is a basic reading skill. Students skim a reading text, usually prior to reading it thoroughly, in order to figure out the main idea.

B. The words that follow are found in the reading on page 5. Match the italicized words in the sentences with their definitions. Place the letter of the definition in the space next to the word. There is one additional definition you will not use.

a. situation; environment

b. develop gradually (little by little)

c. change

d. someone who takes part or shares in something

e. a person from whom others are descended

f. action of watching carefully; noticing

g. difficult

h. acts or practices common to a particular group of people

i. intelligent

1. _____ My *ancestors* are originally from Ireland; my great grandfather came to the U.S. in the 1800s.

2. _____ There are tourist buses downtown that *transform* into boats in order to cross the small lake.

3. _____ One *observation* I have made about Americans is that they are very friendly the first time you meet them.

4. _____ There were more than 50 *participants* in the seminar; the small room was completely full.

5. _____ One *custom* for Halloween in the U.S. is for children to wear costumes and go around to their neighbors "trick or treating."

6. _____ Scientists continue to study how the human body *evolves* (e.g., how people are taller today than in the past).

7. _____ Setting up your new iPod is not very *complex*; the menus tell you exactly what you need to do.

8. _____ It is important to keep the historical *context* of the movie in mind; the clothing and food were popular in the 1700s.

C. Read the passage.

The Study of Humans

Many different types of scientists study human beings, but there is a group of scientists whose job is quite complex. These scientists are called anthropologists, and their job is to understand human behavior, both in the past and present. The word *anthropology* comes from two Greek words. *Anthropos* means "humankind," and *logos* means "word" or "study." Thus, anthropology is a science that can be compared in some ways with other fields of study, such as sociology, psychology, political science, economics, and linguistics. Anthropologists examine the development of the human race by studying our physical characteristics; languages; customs; traditions; and cultural, political, economic, and social institutions.

Anthropology has several different branches: physical anthropology, archaeology, linguistic anthropology, and cultural anthropology. Physical anthropologists try to understand how humans have evolved from their ancestors over the last few million years. They are very similar to modern biologists who study humans. Physical anthropologists, however, study the human body of the past. Archaeologists examine different forms of social organization by looking at how humans lived based on the remains of the houses and objects that humans have left behind. Linguists involved in the field of anthropology are interested in comparing different language forms as well as different uses of language in different contexts. Cultural anthropologists study human behavior and compare different cultures. They usually work in the form of participant observation—they live with the people whom they study for a period of time. Cultural anthropologists who record and analyze data from their participant observations are called ethnographers.

Your participation in this course will transform you into a sort of cultural anthropologist as you learn about a society that practices customs different from your own. If you are studying English in the United States, then you will be working like an ethnographer as you participate in the culture. You will be continuously comparing your culture with American culture as you see how several parts of Americans' lives fit into a way of life as a whole.

D. Use the words in the list that follows, and match them with the correct description.

biological anthropology   linguist   *logos*
archaeologist   ethnographer   cultural anthropologists

1. _____   studies customs

2. _____   type of anthropologist who lives with people within the culture
                                she is studying, taking notes and analyzing her observations

3. _____   type of anthropologist who studies the languages of different
                                societies

4. _____   Greek word meaning "study"

5. _____   type of anthropologist who studies the houses in which
                                people lived in the past

6. _____   another possible term for physical anthropology

E. Fill in the missing parts of the diagram that outlines the field of anthropology. Use these words to fill
   in the different branches and possible subjects of different types of anthropologists.

physical anthropology   religions   storytelling
cultural anthropology   houses   human skeletons

> ### Creating Graphic Organizers
> One way to organize ideas in a reading is by using graphic organizers. The
> diagram organizes the main ideas for you. However, it is usually up to you to
> design your graphic organizer, which means you have to figure out the main
> ideas and details on your own.

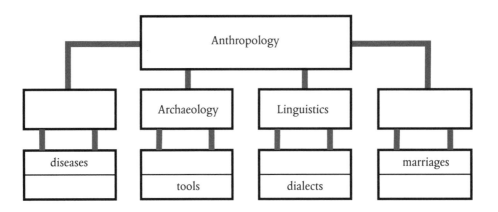

II. Different Views of Learning Culture

A. The title of the next passage you will read is "'BIG-C' and 'LITTLE-c' Culture." What do you think might be some differences between big-C and little-c cultures? Think about the answers to this question as you read the passage about the history of culture learning in foreign language teaching.

"BIG-C" and "LITTLE-c" Culture

Before the 1960s, many foreign language teachers and their students believed that the main reason for learning a foreign language was to know about the history, literature, and art of a particular culture. Because of this narrow viewpoint, learning about a foreign culture usually occurred at high levels of language proficiency, only after students were able to read texts in the second language. At this level, teachers and students usually studied the music, literature, art, history, architecture, etc.—the focus was on the *products* of a culture (what the artists, writers, and music composers created). For many researchers, this type of culture learning is referred to as big-C culture.

During the 1960s, however, communication became the goal of foreign language learning, and teachers started to emphasize some of the anthropological aspects of culture. Nelson Brooks, a researcher in foreign language learning, believes that the study of culture goes beyond artistic expression (e.g., literature, music, and art). He concentrates on the personal side of culture—"the distinctive life-way of a people." He once said, "This aspect of culture is absolutely basic to an understanding of what makes us what we are." With this type of culture learning, teachers and students focus on the *practices* and *communities* of a society—the shared activities, events, groups, *institutions*, etc.). It is also believed that if students concentrate on the everyday patterns of living of people in a particular culture, perhaps students can learn language and culture simultaneously. This type of culture learning is referred to as little-c culture, and most teachers today believe that it can be introduced to students at all levels of language learning.

B. Now, look back at the list of items on page 1 and decide which ones would be considered aspects of big-C culture (artists' creations) and which ones would be parts of little-c culture (patterns of living). Label big-C items with a "C" and little-c items with a "c." It is important to keep in mind that this list is not complete and that there may be some items that you believe are both big-C and little-c aspects.

art (C or c)   family (C or c)   communication (C or c)   music (C or c)
money (C or c)   politics (C or c)   education (C or c)   food (C or c)
television (C or c)   sports (C or c)   history (C or c)   literature (C or c)
movies (C or c)   gestures (C or c)   holidays (C or c)   proverbs/idioms (C or c)
houses (C or c)   cooking (C or c)   language (C or c)   clothing (C or c)

III. Generalizations and Stereotypes

A. Is it possible to characterize an American in just a few words? Using only three adjectives, try to describe an American. Compare your list with other students in class. Did you choose any of the same words as anyone else in your class?

1. _____   2. _____   3. _____

 B. Listen to this famous tale. Fill in the blanks with the words that you hear as you hear them.

The Blind Men and the Elephant

Six blind men and a young _____ went into a forest to find _____ elephant. Obviously, none of the blind men _____ ever seen one, but they wanted _____ find out what an elephant was like. They did _____ really know what to expect. The young child directed the _____ to where an elephant was standing.

The first _____ ran into the side of the elephant and said, "_____ elephant is like a wall."

The second man _____ the tusk of the elephant and said, "This elephant is _____ a spear."

The third man _____ the trunk of the elephant with his hands and _____ , "The elephant is like a snake."

The fourth man _____ the elephant's ear and said, "This elephant is like

_____ fan."

The fifth man reached out _____ hand and felt the elephant's knee and

said, "It's like a _____."

The sixth man grabbed onto _____ tail and said, "This elephant is a rope."

Each of the blind men _____ that his judgment was correct. In fact, the

_____ argued for years, each man insisting that his personal opinion was the

right one.

C. Now reread the tale. What do you think is the message is?

    a. You should never try to touch an elephant.

    b. Our opinions about other people are usually wrong.

    c. Our individual perceptions can lead to misinterpretations.

D. Look back at your list of three adjectives that you chose to describe an American. Do you believe that it is possible to describe an American using only 3 words? 300 words? 3,000 words?

E. Think of two statements that you believe describe Americans. Write those statements here, and compare them with other students in the class.

    1. _____

    2. _____

F. Do you think that these statements are true about all Americans? Read the passage that follows and decide whether your statements are stereotypes or facts.

Stereotypes

When we observe other people, we often form opinions about their values and behavior, usually focusing on the fact that they are "different" from us. As you study the material in this textbook, you will often be asked to compare your culture with American culture, and it will be very natural for you to use your own culture as a basis of comparison. You will be considering why you act the way you do in certain situations, and you will also start considering why Americans act the way they do in certain situations. You will soon understand how important it is to avoid stereotyping.

A stereotype is a belief about another person or group of people. Stereotypes are usually oversimplified descriptions based on only one or two characteristics, and even though they can seem either favorable or unfavorable, stereotypes about ethnic groups are often insulting. People often stereotype others based on images they have seen or heard in movies, on television, or from other people. They may judge others because of differences in ethnic, political, economic, or religious backgrounds. During your study of American culture, it is very important that you do not use stereotypes to describe Americans. Therefore, if you have seen several Americans acting a certain way and you assume that all people from that group always act like that, then you are stereotyping.

You will also be learning several facts and generalizations about Americans and the culture. Facts are supported by research that uses ways of measuring things. These facts will help you avoid stereotyping people and will help you to better understand the American lifestyle.

G. In your own words, write a definition for the words *stereotype* and *fact*.

1. stereotype _____.

2. fact _____.

H. Read each sentence, and decide whether each one is a stereotype (S) or fact (F).

1. _____   Americans eat too many hamburgers, pizza, and sandwiches.

2. _____   More than 60 percent of Americans 20 years and older are overweight, according to the Centers for Disease Control.

3. _____   Young Americans generally leave their parents' home at age 18.

4. _____   Americans eat too many candy bars.

5. _____   Americans smile at everyone on the street.

6. _____   According to the U.S. Bureau of Labor Statistics, 98 percent of American pre-school and kindergarten teachers are female.

7. _____   Hispanic-Americans include people with Spanish, Mexican, or Latin American ethnic origins.

I. Look at this sentence. Is this sentence a stereotype? Why or why not?

Many Americans like to eat at McDonald's®.

Using Qualifiers

Certain words are used in English to indicate that the statement is true most of the time, but not always. These are called **qualifiers.**

generally speaking	it is often the case
generally	frequently
often	perhaps
may	many

J. Rewrite each sentence, changing it from a stereotype to a general statement and using a qualifier from the language box.

> Example: *Americans are always too busy.* (stereotype)
> *Americans are often very busy.* (general statement)

1. All Americans go to baseball games during their lifetimes.

   _____

2. American people eat dinner too early.

   _____

3. Americans eat too much junk food every day.

   _____

4. Americans smile at people they don't even know.

   _____

Distinguishing between *too* and *very*

Do not confuse these two adverbs! *Very* is used with adjectives to make them stronger—to a greater degree. *Too* is negative—to an undesirable degree.

The box is very heavy.   The box is too heavy.

K. A list of adjectives that are sometimes used to describe people follows. Working with a partner, think of an antonym (a word that means the opposite) for each given word.

Example: cheap _____ *expensive* _____

1. tall _____

2. outgoing _____

3. private _____

4. helpful _____

5. aggressive _____

6. independent _____

7. quiet _____

8. hard-working _____

Making Comparisons

When we want to compare two things using adjectives or adverbs, which is often done when we are making generalizations, we use the comparative forms. For example, look at this sentence:

In general, American cars are larger than cars in my country.

To form the comparative for one-syllable adjectives or two-syllable adjectives ending in -y, add -er to the regular form (change -y to i before adding -er).

cheap / cheaper   lazy / lazier
long / longer   easy / easier

To form the comparative for longer adjectives and adverbs that end with -ly, add the word *more* before the adjective or adverb.

quickly / more quickly   peaceful / more peaceful
loud / more loudly   carefully / more carefully

A small group of fairly common adjectives and adverbs form their comparatives in irregular ways:

good / better   bad / worse
many / more   much / more
some / more   little / less or littler
well / better   badly / worse

When you are comparing two things that are similar, you can use *as X as.*

In general, students in the U.S. seem to be as hard-working as students in my country.

L. Now, write sentences comparing Americans with people from your culture using the adjectives given. Remember to use a qualifier to avoid stereotyping. Refer to the language box on making comparisons on page 13.

Example: *Generally speaking, American cars are cheaper than cars in my country.*

1. tall   _____

2. outgoing   _____

3. private   _____

4. helpful   _____

5. aggressive   _____

6. independent   _____

7. quiet   _____

8. hard-working _____

IV. How to Talk about Culture

Now that we have looked at stereotypes and the dangers of overgeneralizing, we can focus on how to express our opinions more effectively. Expressing your opinion is not always easy to do, especially when you are surrounded by other students. Throughout this course, however, you will often be asked your opinion about your own culture and American culture.

A. Read this conversation.

Bill: I downloaded the new Harry Potter movie yesterday. I think that it's one of the worst movies I've ever seen!

Juan: I couldn't agree more! I rented the DVD a couple weeks ago, and I really didn't like it.

Carlos: You both have a right to your opinion, but if you ask me, you just have to watch Harry Potter movies in the movie theater. I thought the special effects were great. The technology used to make that movie was very advanced. The point I'm making is that action movies are not as good on video as on the big movie screens with stereo sound.

Bill: You could be right, but don't you think the acting was bad, too?

Juan: You can say that again!

Carlos: Are you kidding? You have to remember that the actors had to imagine they were surrounded by characters created by computers.

Bill: Well, I respect your opinion. Maybe I do have to see it on a big movie screen instead of on my video iPod.

B. Reread the conversation, and underline all the phrases that express opinion, agreement, and disagreement.

Expressing Opinions

Some different expressions that can be used to let a person know your opinion of a topic follow.

The point I'm making is . . .	*In my opinion . . .*
I believe . . .	*I think that . . .*
I feel that . . .	*As I see it . . .*
Don't you think that . . .	
It seems to me that . . .	*According to . . .*
If you ask me . . .	*Personally, I think . . .*

Agreeing

Agreeing with someone is a lot easier than disagreeing. Americans use several different expressions.

I couldn't agree more!	*Absolutely!*
How true!	*That's exactly what I was thinking!*
You're exactly right!	*Definitely!*
You're right.	*That's true.*
I agree.	*That's a good point.*
You can say that again!	*You bet!*
For sure!	*I'll say!*

Disagreeing

Disagreeing with someone is usually more difficult. You have to be aware of the relationship between you and the person with whom you are disagreeing. There are both direct and indirect expressions.

You've got to be joking/kidding!	*Don't make me laugh!*
I disagree with what you are saying.	*I respect your opinion, but . . .*
I'm afraid I disagree.	*I'm not sure I agree.*
Maybe, but . . .	*I don't agree.*
I don't see it that way.	*Don't be ridiculous!*
Are you crazy?	*Well, you have a right to your opinion, but . . .*
I don't think so.	*You could be right, but don't you think that . . . ?*
You're nuts.	*What a joke!*

C. Reread the expressions used to disagree. Which ones are direct, and which are indirect? Where do you think each expression would go on the direct-indirect scale?

```
<——————————————————————————————————————————————————>
1           2           3           4           5           6           7           8
Direct                                                                      Indirect
Are you crazy?                                                              Maybe, but . . .
```

D. With a partner, review the conversation in Activity A on pages 14–15. Replace the phrases of opinions, agreement, and disagreement with other expressions from the language box on page 15.

E. Some opinions follow. Respond to them in three different ways: (1) agree with the statement; (2) disagree with the statement directly; (3) disagree with the statement but soften it by making it more indirect. Remember to support your disagreement with a reason.

Example: Don't you think that Brad Pitt is a good actor?

Agree: Absolutely! He's also pretty good-looking!

Disagree (directly):   You must be joking! All of his movies are the same!

Disagree (indirectly):   Well, you have a right to your opinion, but I don't think he's very talented.

1. *Personally, I think American food is really good.*

   Agree: _____

   Disagree (directly): _____

   Disagree (indirectly): _____

2. *In my opinion, traveling to other countries is a waste of money.*

   Agree: _____

   Disagree (directly): _____

   Disagree (indirectly): _____

3. *If you ask me, McDonald's® has the best hamburgers in the world.*

   Agree: _____

   Disagree (directly): _____

   Disagree (indirectly): _____

4. *American baseball is so incredibly boring.*

   Agree: _____

   Disagree (directly): _____

   Disagree (indirectly): _____

5. *Don't you think summer is the best season of the year?*

   Agree: _____

   Disagree (directly): _____

   Disagree (indirectly): _____

V. Values Application

A. People from different cultures have different values. There are several of these values that we can use to generally describe people from different cultures. Look at the values listed and try to match their characteristics.

1. individualistic _____   a. not hidden; easily understood

2. cooperative _____   b. having a great interest in possessions, money, etc.

3. direct _____   c. same in value, rank, etc.

4. informal _____   d. working together

5. equal _____   e. based on past principles, beliefs, etc.

6. traditional _____   f. casual; not formal

7. competitive _____   g. independent in thought or actions

8. materialistic _____   h. having strong desire to be the best and succeed, usually on an individual basis

9. practical / efficient _____ i. moving forward or developing continuously

10. private _____   j. not casual

11. progressive _____   k. personal; not to be shared with others

12. formal _____   l. effective; convenient; working well without waste

B. Check the box that corresponds to the correct word form of the values.

	Noun (Person)	Noun (Thing)	Verb	Adjective	Adverb
individualism					
cooperation					
directly					
informal					
equality					
tradition					
competitor					
materialism					
practicality					
efficiency					
private					
progress					
formally					

C. Some situations that demonstrate some of the values listed follow. Match each situation or belief with the corresponding value.

Situation	Corresponding Value(s)
1. A student in your history class does not seem comfortable letting you borrow her notes from the lecture because she is afraid that you might do better than she does on the next exam.	
2. Your next door neighbor often spends money on new stereo and video equipment. He also usually buys a new car every three or four years.	
3. You just heard one of your classmates call your professor by her first name.	
4. One day after history class, a student asks if you would like to join a study group to prepare for tomorrow's exam.	
5. People donate thousands of dollars to an organization that will be sending scientists to live on the planet Mars in the year 2025.	
6. A manager of a small company prefers that her employees call and refer to her as "Ms. Mead."	
7. A recent high school graduate will attend college this fall. She has saved money from working part-time during high school and plans to continue working part-time during college.	

D. Expressions and slogans (short advertising phrases) common in the United States follow. Which value(s) do you think each one reflects?

    a. competition

    b. individualism

    c. materialism

    d. directness

    e. progress

    1. _____ "I did it my way."

    2. _____ "It's the future that counts."

    3. _____ "History doesn't matter."

    4. _____ "Tell it like it is."

    5. _____ "Look out for number one."

    6. _____ "Do your own thing."

    7. _____ "Have it your own way."

    8. _____ "Bigger is better."

    9. _____ "Time is money."

  10. _____ "Shop 'til you drop."

  11. _____ "Just do it."

  12. _____ "Rules are made to be broken."

E. There are some obvious reasons for expecting people from a similar culture to act and think similarly, but there are other less obvious factors that are also important to consider. Look at the chart. Scan the reading on pages 23–24, and fill in the chart with the appropriate information about the United States. Then, based on your own knowledge, fill in as much of the chart as possible about your country. Ignore the values column for now.

Factors Affecting Culture	Your Country	United States	Value(s)
Geographical Location			
Size			
Foundation of the Government			
When Country Was Founded			
Religious Background			

Scanning

A reading skill called scanning is used when you are looking for specific information in a reading passage. You do not read every word in the text; in fact, it is not important to understand every word in the text. All you want to do is find the necessary information. For example, think about when you read a newspaper in your native language. You might find an interesting article, but you probably do not read every word. Instead, you usually look for information such as when, how, or why something happened. Scanning is therefore done at a very high speed.

F. Carefully read the article on values.

The Formation of Values in a Society

People from the same culture share several similar values. People evaluate (judge) objects, events, and behavior based on their values. How are these values formed? Let's look at some geographical, historical, and religious factors that have affected the value system in the United States.

Some factors that are important to the basis of values concern the geography of the country. The United States is the fourth largest nation in the world, covering 3,536,278 square miles (9,159,123 square kilometers). The amount of natural resources, including the land, fresh water, and animals, is abundant. The United States comprises, or makes up, a very large part of the North American continent. It is bordered by two large oceans and only two other countries, Mexico and Canada. If you drove the 2,825 miles (4,546 kilometers) from New York City to Los Angeles, it would take you at least 4–5 days, even if you only stopped to sleep, eat, and fill up your gas tank.

Second, several historical factors play an important role in the American value system. The United States was founded by a revolution; the early settlers of the United States opposed the tyranny, which is control with complete power, of many European rulers. The government was thus founded by settlers who had escaped controlling kings, churches, priests, and aristocrats. The new citizens of the United States put the power in the hands of the people by electing representatives to establish the laws and the foreign policy. This democracy is the oldest in the world, even though the country did not become established until 1776.

Last, at that time in Europe, there were major religious conflicts, or struggles, between Catholics and Protestants. Many people escaped from some of these European countries to the North American continent in order to have religious freedom. In fact, persecution—causing one to suffer for religious or political beliefs—was a major reason why many Protestants left different parts of Europe in the 17th century. Today, the existence of many Protestant denominations, such as Presbyterian, Baptist, Methodist, Lutheran, Episcopalian, reveal the religious diversity that developed in the United States. No one single church <u>dominates,</u> or controls, because the emphasis is on the individual and not one particular religion; the development of the United States was very much influenced by this emphasis on the individual.

Because of the diversity of the United States, it is impossible to claim that all Americans hold the same values. However, the large size of the country may cause many people to value their privacy and space. In addition, the historical and religious factors may help explain why many Americans are considered to be individualistic. Nevertheless, the development of any country is always in a state of <u>flux</u> (change), and although there are many factors that contribute to shaping cultural values, the geographical, historical, and religious factors are important to the change and growth of a country.

G. In order to understand the passage better, you need to know the meaning of many new words. Look at the sentence that follows. Based on the information in the sentence, what is the definition of the italicized word? What clues did you use to do this?

"People *evaluate* (judge), objects, events, and behavior based on their values."

Finding Definitions in a Text

Many times when you read something, the writer will provide a definition for certain vocabulary by using clues or phrases. Look at the examples that follow:

    a. Values, which are shared ideas or standards, are usually similar among people in the same culture."

In this example, the word *value* is defined by using the simple present tense of the verb *be*.

    An author will often use certain punctuation to help define words within a sentence. Look at these two examples:

    b. The *pope* (leader of the Roman Catholic Church) acts as the bishop of Rome.

    c. Persecution—causing one to suffer for religious or political beliefs— was a major reason why many Protestants left different parts of Europe in the 17th century.

In the two sentences above, parentheses and dashes are used to help define words that an author believes need to be defined.

    Sometimes, the word is not clearly defined, but the writer provides an example that helps you make an intelligent guess about the meaning.

    d. Different climates in the United States, **such as** tropical, temperate, dry, and cold, also contribute to the diversity of lifestyles of Americans.

In this sentence the writer has given the examples of several different weather conditions to represent the word *climates*. The language clue, such as, is boldfaced.

H. Find these underlined words in the reading on pages 23–24. Circle which of the language clue(s) you used and then write the definition of the word.

Word	Language/Punctuation Clue	Definition
persecution	Verb *to be* Parentheses (Dashes or commas) Example (*such as, for example, etc.*)	causing one to suffer for religious or political beliefs
comprises	Verb *to be* Parentheses Dashes or commas Example (*such as, for example, etc.*)	
tyranny	Verb *to be* Parentheses Dashes or commas Example (*such as, for example, etc.*)	
conflicts	Verb *to be* Parentheses Dashes or commas Example (*such as, for example, etc.*)	
denominations	Verb *to be* Parentheses Dashes or commas Example (*such as, for example, etc.*)	
dominates	Verb *to be* Parentheses Dashes or commas Example (*such as, for example, etc.*)	
flux	Verb *to be* Parentheses Dashes or commas Example (*such as, for example, etc.*)	

I. Look back to the chart on page 22. Look at each of the factors again and based on what you learned in the reading, fill in the appropriate value(s).

CHAPTER 2

Speaking Out

How Americans Communicate

Look at these pictures of Americans talking. Also, think about other Americans that you have recently observed in person or on television and consider these questions.

- What do you think the people in the photos are talking about?
- What do you observe about Americans and the way that they talk to one another (volume, distance, taking turns, etc.)? How is the way people talk to each other in the United States different from your own culture?

Culture influences the way people communicate with one another. Misunderstandings can occur between people of different cultures simply due to different patterns of conversation, subjects, and styles. This chapter discusses the American style of communication so you can avoid making wrong judgments about Americans and avoid being wrongly judged by Americans. In addition, you will be able to see how values are reflected in the way Americans communicate.

This chapter looks at certain aspects of communication, both verbal and nonverbal. Greetings (both formal and informal) and maintaining conversation with small talk as well as gestures and body language are considered important in learning to communicate in another language. The American style of these conversational tools may be very different from your own culture's. You will also practice language skills, including:

- using techniques to learn syllable stress
- recognizing appropriate forms of address; recognizing introductions, greetings, and farewells
- listening for the main topic and specific details
- asking questions
- using modals of advice and suggestion
- recognizing different forms of conditionals
- predicting and previewing the topic of reading
- learning the meaning of idiomatic expressions

After completing this chapter, return to this page and assess how well you did in reaching these objectives.

Vocabulary Development

When words in English have more than one syllable, the word is pronounced with stress on one of the syllables. In the word *introvert*, there are three syllables, and the stress is on the first syllable:

in tro vert

● ○ ○

Listen to your teacher pronounce the words in the vocabulary list for this chapter, and fill in the circle for the syllable that has the stress. Then, review the list, and put a check (✔) next to the words you know. When you are finished with the chapter, return to this list and make sure you can put a check next to all of the words.

gesture ____	○○	compliment ____	○○○
communication ____	○○○○○	greeting ____	○○
aware ____	○○	encounter ____	○○○
interaction ____	○○○○	facial ____	○○
introduction ____	○○○○	expression ____	○○○
proxemics ____	○○○	universal ____	○○○○
integrity ____	○○○○	extrovert ____	○○○
reveal ____	○○	cluster ____	○○
consultant ____	○○○	interpret ____	○○○
occupation ____	○○○○	professional ____	○○○○
constant ____	○○	focus ____	○○
financial ____	○○○	contact ____	○○
feature ____	○○	environment ____	○○○○
physical ____	○○○	significant ____	○○○○

Using Techniques to Learn Syllable Stress of New Words

There are different techniques you can use to help yourself learn to "hear" syllable stress. Some students are more visual, and seeing the word stress like this ● ○ ○ is helpful. For other students, it helps to **hear** and **feel** the word stress. For example, you can tap on a table, clap your hands, snap your fingers, or stretch a rubber band on the stressed syllable of a word to help you "feel" the stress more.

I. Introductions and Other Encounters

A. Look at the chart that follows. Imagine you have to address these people (on the phone, in person, etc.). Which of the following titles would you use: Mr., Ms., Mrs., Professor, Dr., Senator/President, or no title at all?

Person / Situation	
1. Your former high school teacher named David Johnson	Mr. Johnson
2. President of the U.S. named David Geiss	
3. Child you baby-sit named John Adams	
4. History professor named Luck Pickering	
5. Colleague at work named Robert Ricci	
6. Senator of North Carolina named Heather Boldt	

Using Forms of Address in Academic Settings

If you are studying in the United States, you have probably met a variety of instructors with different styles, some more informal than others. Even though informality is quite common in the United States, you should not assume that it is okay to call your instructors by their first names only, even if they are younger than you. In addition, it is considered impolite to call instructors by their last name only (i.e., in the preceding chart, for example, #5, "Pickering" would be considered unacceptable).

On the first day of class, it is important that you listen carefully to find out how your professors want to be addressed. Also, if you are not sure whether or not your professor has a Ph.D., you should assume that he or she does and use the title *Dr.* or *Professor* when addressing your instructor in person, by email, and on the phone, etc.

There are three different titles used by women: *Ms., Miss, and Mrs.* *Ms.* is the **safest** choice since you do not know which title the woman prefers or whether she is married or unmarried. In general, it's best to choose a neutral title and wait for a person to say, *Please call me X.*

B. After you meet a person, you might have to introduce that person to someone else that you already know. Rank the expressions that Americans use to introduce others, including common responses, from the most formal (1) to the most informal (4).

Introduction	Response
_____ Mitch, Susan, . . . Susan, Mitch.	Hi.
_____ I'd like to introduce Dr. Jim Michaels.	How do you do?
_____ This is one of my colleagues, Tom Byrd.	Nice to meet you.
_____ I'd like you to meet Nelson.	It's a pleasure to meet you.

The ways that people use their bodies to greet one another may also differ, depending on the formality of the situation. In fact, these may also vary within one culture. A firm handshake and direct eye contact are the common first-time greeting in the United States because they reflect honesty and directness.

As relationships between people change, greetings between friends of the same gender and of different gender can vary. The American style of greetings between friends may be very different from your culture. In addition, it is important to consider the ethnic diversity of the United States and realize that many nationalities have brought their customs here and continue to practice them.

C. What people say and how they use their bodies in greetings and conversations vary based on the relationship and cultural background. Interview an American and someone from a country different from your own, and fill in the chart. Record the amount of space (proxemics), the type of greeting (verbal / physical), and the eye contact. Keep in mind that these are generalizations only since you are only interviewing one person from each cultural background.

Relationship	Proxemics (the space between people)	Greeting (what do they do, what do they say)	Eye Contact
You and your boss			
American			
Person from _____			
People from your cultural background			
You and a government leader (e.g., governor)			
American			
Person from _____			
People from your cultural background			
You and your best friend			
American			
Person from _____			
People from your cultural background			

D. In your chart in Activity C, did you and your classmates record any of these following greetings?

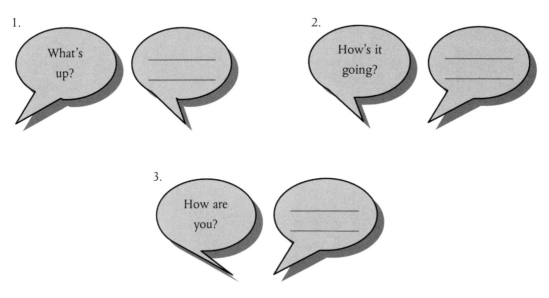

1.
What's up?
_____
_____

2.
How's it going?
_____
_____

3.
How are you?
_____
_____

Fill in appropriate responses to these greetings.

E. Some situations in which you might greet or say good-bye to another person follow. What would you say in English in each case?

1. Saying good night to a child. _____

2. Saying good-bye after a job interview. _____

3. Going to a professor's office for help with a problem. _____

_____

4. Saying good-bye to your teacher at the end of class. _____

_____

5. Saying hello to a good friend. _____

II. American Conversation

 A. Listen to a dialogue between Jan and Greg, and answer the questions.

1. What kind of relationship do Jan and Greg have?

   a. brother-sister

   b. boyfriend-girlfriend

   c. new acquaintances

2. What is the topic of the conversation?

   a. sports

   b. work

   c. hometowns

3. Does either Jan or Greg dominate, or control, the conversation?

4. What do Jan or Greg have in common?

5. Jan and Greg are involved in a **small talk** conversation. What do you think small talk means? Why do you think Americans use **small** to describe this kind of conversation?

B. In groups of three or four, make lists of topics that you think might be acceptable and unacceptable for small talk between Americans.

Acceptable Topics	Unacceptable Topics

C. Scan this following passage about small talk. Look for additional acceptable and unacceptable topics for small talk, and add them to your list in the previous activity.

American Small Talk

When Americans meet one another for the first time, they begin their conversation with "small talk." The topics of these conversations are very general and often situational—people start talking about anything in their common physical environment, such as the weather, the room in which they are standing or sitting, the food that they are eating, etc. Small talk is important because Americans are not very comfortable with silence. It is important, however, to know which topics are acceptable (safe) and which are unacceptable (unsafe) in American culture. Until Americans get to know one another better, certain acceptable small talk topics are usually the focus of conversations.

Situational topics like the weather are acceptable in many cultures, but they obviously cannot be discussed for a long period of time. Asking someone about his or her occupation is also very common, especially for Americans, who place a high value on working. Questions about one's preferences or tastes could also be asked. For example, one could ask a person if she has heard the latest single by Beyoncé or Usher, which may lead to a longer discussion about musical preferences. Compliments are common conversation starters. For example, someone might start a conversation by saying, "That's a cool bag. Where did you get it?" Last, in a country like the United States where people move often, places of origin are often discussed, and non-native students will probably be asked by Americans about their country and their impressions of the United States.

There are many topics, however, that are inappropriate to use in starting conversation. For example, religion is considered a very personal matter. One could ask about general religious practices in the United States, but in general people must not ask others directly about their personal religious practices during small talk. Politics is usually another unacceptable topic. Americans tend to avoid the subject, especially if it is obvious that all parties do not have the same beliefs. Two other subjects will immediately make Americans uncomfortable: age and money. Americans value youth, so many Americans want to keep their age a secret, especially women. Regarding financial matters, income and the price of possessions are also personal matters and should not be used to start a conversation with an American. For example, if you compliment someone on her sweater or shoes, you should not ask the cost of the items because that would be inappropriate.

Being aware of these acceptable and unacceptable topics may help people from other cultures feel more comfortable around Americans that they meet for the first time. Listening to American small talk has often led non-native speakers to make wrong judgments about an American's ability or desire to carry on a conversation because the topics seem impersonal and the conversations are short. Culture, however, influences the way that people communicate with one another. Learning about this feature of conversation will help you understand Americans better.

D. Write three questions about appropriate topics that you might ask someone you are meeting for the first time.

Example: (weather) *What do you think about this hot weather?*

1. _____

2. _____

3. _____

 E. Listen to each dialogue, and list the topic(s) of each conversation. Then decide whether the entire small talk conversation is acceptable (safe) or unacceptable (unsafe).

1. Topic _____ A or U

2. Topic _____ A or U

3. Topic _____ A or U

4. Topic _____ A or U

F. When giving someone advice, *must*, *should*, and *could* are often used. Look back at the reading on American Small Talk, and underline the sentences containing these words. What is the difference between *must*, *should*, and *could*?

Using Modals of Advice or Suggestion

These modals are followed by the simple form of the verb.

Example:	"He doesn't ask their ages." → "He should never ask their ages."
should	Something is advised, but you make the choice. "You should try to meet more people."
should not	It is advised that you not do something. The contraction is *shouldn't*. "He should not call her by her first name."
must not (very strong)	Something is prohibited. It is very important that you not do something. The contraction is *mustn't*. "You mustn't be too afraid to meet people."
could	Something is suggested as a possible future action. "She could ask him to dinner on Friday."

G. Reread the passage on American Small Talk. Write an email message to a friend at home explaining how to make small talk with Americans. Remember to mention the acceptable and unacceptable topics. You should use various modals in your message.

You could (ask / inquire about / talk about) . . . .

You should . . . .

You should not (ask / inquire about / talk about) . . . .

You must not . . . .

H. Maintaining a balance in a conversation with Americans is also important. Americans become uncomfortable if people ask too many questions, and they become frustrated if their own questions are repeatedly answered with only one- or two-word responses. Listen to this dialogue between two students. Think about the questions as you listen.

1. What is the topic of the conversation? Is it acceptable or unacceptable?

_____

_____

2. Why does John decide to stop talking to Amy?

_____

_____

3. What should Amy have done to make the conversation more successful?

_____

_____

I. Read the text of the conversation that you heard between John and Amy. With a partner, use suggestions, and change the dialogue so that it is a successful example of American small talk.

John: Hi! You're in English 406 with Dr. McGorman, aren't you?

Amy: Yeah. She's a really great professor; I love that class.

John: I do too. Do you like that novel we're reading now?

Amy: Not really. _____.

_____?

John: _____.

Are you an English major?

Amy: Yes. _____.

_____?

John: _____.

How long have you been at Morton College?

Amy: Two years. _____.

_____?

III. Nonverbal Communication

A. Read the quotation, and answer the questions.

A person cannot not communicate. Though she may decide to stop talking, it is impossible for her to stop behaving. The behavior of a person—her facial expressions, posture, gestures, and other actions—provides an uninterrupted stream of information and a constant source of clues to the feelings she is experiencing. The reading of body language, therefore, is one of the most significant skills of good listening. (Robert Bolton, *People Skills*, New York: Simon & Schuster, 1979, 78.)

1. What do you think "a person cannot not communicate" means?

_____

_____

2. What types of behavior make up nonverbal communication?

_____

_____

3. Why should you pay attention to someone's body language?

_____

_____

B. Look at the title of the newspaper article on page 42. Based on the title and what you have learned so far in this chapter, what do you predict this reading will be about? Write any words or phrases in the space that represent what the text will be about.

_____

_____

_____

Predicting and Previewing a Reading

You have just used one reading skill: **predicting.** Another reading skill is **previewing.** Both skills give you enough information about the text so that you begin to think about it and form opinions about it. Then when you read the text, you understand it better. Predicting and previewing can help you to read more effectively.

C. Now preview the text by reading it as quickly as possible. You can do this by reading the title, the subheadings, and the first sentence of every paragraph. Write all the vocabulary and the ideas that you remember.

_____   _____

_____   _____

_____   _____

Actions Speak Louder Than Words

Body language can give away hidden feelings

By Carla Wheeler & Carla Clarkson
Gannett News Service

Bodies gab. And they usually speak louder than words.

The way people cross their ankles, shake your hand, smile and fold their arms says a lot about them, says Phil Miller, a consultant in Fullerton, Calif., who conducts workshops on body language.

"The body does what the mind is thinking," says Miller, who started to study body signals more than 40 years ago while serving in the Marines. "Your body always says something. People who read body language can pick up what your true feelings are."

Knowing the meaning behind someone's body moves and learning how to put your best body language forward can help you personally and professionally, according to Miller, who also works with politicians as an image consultant.

For example, if you're a salesperson and a client you've just met allows you into what they consider their personal space, it might be OK to try to close the sale, Miller says. A person's personal space is usually 3½ feet to the front, 18 inches to the back, and six inches to each side, he says.

"If someone will allow you in their space, they're beginning to trust you," Miller says.

Another way to find out if someone likes or trusts you is to look at the pupils of their eyes, Miller says. If a person is interested in you or what you're saying, the pupils of their eyes will get bigger, he says. "If the pupils get smaller, it's the opposite—they don't like you or what you're talking about," Miller says. There are two basic body positions—open

WHAT IT MEANS

- Pursing the lips: Disapproval or concentration
- Licking the lips: Nervousness
- Biting the lip: Self-reproach
- Tapping the foot: Nervousness, impatience, or annoyance
- Tilting the head to one side: Sympathy; she's listening closely
- Looking at you sideways: Mistrust
- Putting the hands behind the back: Uncomfortable or defensive, afraid of what she might reveal

and closed—which are key indicators of a person's feelings, says Dr. Judith Grasier, clinical psychologist in Washington, D.C.

"Often people are revealing a position and they aren't even aware of it."

A person in a closed position usually will lean away, cross their arms and legs and try to distance themselves from the person they are talking to, Grasier said.

When a person is talking with their body in an open position, they are leaning forward and are relaxed.

Experts agree that a person should never be judged by one sign alone, such as interpreting legs or arms that are crossed.

Terry Williams of the Terry Williams Agency, a public relations firm in New York, says body language is important when interacting with another person or a business.

"If you are confident and truthful, you will be open and direct as far as your body language is concerned," she says. "When there are a cluster of closed positions used, there may be a question of a person's confidence and integrity."

Source: Gannett News Service.

D. Carefully read Actions Speak Louder than Words, and answer the questions based on the article.

1. According to Miller, how can knowing the meaning behind someone's body moves and learning how to put your best body language forward help you?

   _____

   _____

   _____

2. What is a person's desirable personal space?

   _____

   _____

   _____

3. What does it mean if someone allows you into their personal space?

   _____

   _____

   _____

4. What are the two basic body positions?

   _____

   _____

   _____

E. Match each word from the reading with its definition.

gab	consultant	cluster	pick up
integrity	close the sale	pupil	reveal

1. _____ a person who gives professional advice to others

2. _____ to talk continuously (informal)

3. _____ a number of things of the same kind being together

4. _____ to notice

5. _____ to settle; to complete something

6. _____ the small black round opening in the middle of the eye

7. _____ honesty; trustworthiness

8. _____ to show; to make known

Using Conditionals in Future Predictive Clauses

If clauses often express a time in the future, but they can use the present tense. This sentence expresses a condition that predicts a future situation, not necessarily a general fact or habit:

If a person crosses her ankles, she may be afraid.

Notice that the result clause *(she may be afraid)* uses a modal *(may)* with a simple verb *(be)*. Remember, *will* shows that the result is certain if the condition is met, and *may, might,* and *could* show that the result is possible.

Fill in the missing verbs of the sentences from the article.

1. If you're a salesperson and a client you've just met allows you into what they consider their personal space, it _____ okay to try to close the sale.

2. If a person is interested in what you're saying, the pupils of their eyes _____ bigger.

3. If you are confident and truthful, you _____ open and direct as far as your body language is concerned.

F. Read the box "What It Means" in the newspaper article on page 42. Write sentences using future predictive clauses based on the nonverbal clues and emotions given. You may need to change nouns into verbs or adjectives.

Example: *If a person purses her lips, she might disapprove of something.*

1. _____

2. _____

3. _____

4. _____

5. _____

6. _____

G. Answer the questions.

1. Do you think you are a private, shy, quiet (introverted) person? Do you think you are an outgoing and talkative (extroverted) person?

2. Do you think about things in terms of words and numbers or in words and pictures?

3. Which types of careers are you more drawn to: (1) research, law, accounting, engineering, and politics, (2) or art, music, writing, acting, and nursing?

H. Cross your arms in front of your chest, and then look at the diagram that follows. Does the way you cross your arms give clues to your personality?

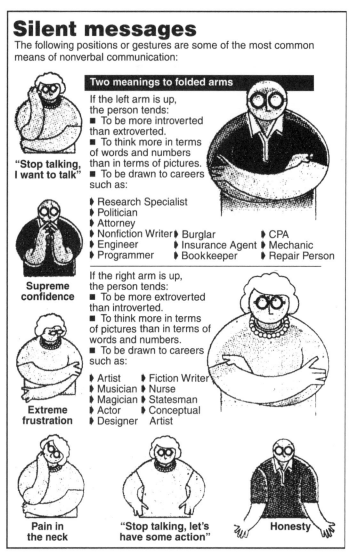

Source: Gannett News Service.

I. Human beings often use their hands and faces to express meaning. These movements are called **gestures.** Gestures are not universal; certain gestures have the exact opposite meaning in different cultures. The body language of cultures is therefore a very important one to learn. Several of the most well-meaning American gestures can often offend those from other countries. Can you match each gesture with its appropriate meaning?

a.   b.   c.   d.

e.   f.   g.   h.

1. _____ "I don't know."

2. _____ "That's great!"

3. _____ "I didn't hear you."

4. _____ "Be quiet."

5. _____ "Call me later."

6. _____ "Oh, no! I forgot."

7. _____ "Good luck."

8. _____ "Okay."

J. There are also many idioms in English that use parts of the body to express an idea. What do you think *keep your chin up* means? Can you think of some idioms or proverbs in your language that use parts of the body to express meaning?

_____

_____

K. Work with a partner, and try to match these idioms with their meanings.

a. tongue-tied	e. foot the bill	i. see eye to eye
b. by heart	f. put our heads together	j. get on my nerves
c. pay through the nose	g. bend over backwards	k. have butterflies (in my stomach)
d. sight for sore eyes	h. eyesore	l. give me a hand

1. _____ agree on something

2. _____ something you are happy or relieved to see

3. _____ to be very nervous

4. _____ to help someone

5. _____ to annoy

6. _____ to spend too much money for something

7. _____ to try really hard to do something

8. _____ to work together on a problem or project

9. _____ unable to talk

10. _____ to pay for something

11. _____ something that is very ugly

12. _____ memorized

L. Use these expressions in the sentences that follow. Be sure to change the verb tenses, agreement, and pronouns when necessary.

1. My son's English teacher does everything she can for her students. She _____ to make sure that the students understand everything.

2. I had to learn all the new vocabulary words _____ for the quiz tomorrow.

3. "If we _____," Amy said, "we will be able to finish the plan for the new park by tomorrow."

4. It was a _____ when the train finally arrived after a four hour delay.

5. You're going to_____ for an apartment in New York City near the park!

6. When the teacher asked Andy to stand up in front of the class and explain the answer to the math problem, he got very nervous and became _____.

7. That old house is such a(n) _____; it hasn't been painted in 50 years and the roof is falling in.

8. I had _____ just before my first job interview, but after I started talking, I became more confident.

9. My boss and I do not _____ on the decision to decrease salaries, but she believes it's the only way to save jobs.

10. I started to take out my wallet to pay for dinner, but my friend said, "Don't worry, I'll _____."

11. It really _____ when teachers assign a lot of homework on Fridays.

12. Can you _____ with moving the computer into my room?

M. Are any of these expressions similar to one in your own language? Which ones? Can you describe in English a popular expression that is not on the list?

_____

_____

_____

_____

IV. Values Application

Some statements that describe American conversation follow. Decide which American value(s) each one represents. Choose among the values discussed in Chapter 1. One has been done for you as an example.

Statement	Value
1. Salary is an unsafe topic in American small talk.	privacy
2. Conversation between two people is like a ping-pong game.	
3. Even though you should not call your professors by their first names immediately, some of them prefer it.	
4. Americans usually stand about 3.5 feet away from each other.	
5. Americans may think you are not paying attention if you do not look directly into their eyes.	

Working Out:

Sports and Fitness in the United States

Match each team name with the correct description based on the history or background of the team.

History/Description	Team Name
1. _____ baseball team named after the two neighboring cities in Minnesota	a. Houston Astros
2. _____ football team originally named the Pirates (same as the baseball team) and then renamed to reflect the steel industy of this city	b. San Francisco 49ers
3. _____ baseball team renamed in 1965 after the new NASA Space Center in this city	c. Indiana Pacers
4. _____ basketball team named after the front car at the most famous auto race, Indianapolis 500	d. Minneapolis Twins
5. _____ baseball team named in 1970 after the beer breweries famous in this urban area	e. Seattle Supersonics
6. _____ basketball team that joined the NBA in 1967; the team was named after a jet that Boeing was working on to compete with the Concorde	f. Milwaukee Brewers
7. _____ football team named after the pioneers of the gold rush of 1849 that took place east of this California city	g. Colorado Rockies
8. _____ football team, originally located in Boston, named to honor this area's history as the birthplace of the American Revolution	h. New Orleans Saints
9. _____ football team whose name is based on the date it joined the NFL (November 1, 1966, All Saints' Day) and is located in a city famous for jazz and the song "When the Saints Go Marching In"	i. New England Patriots
10. _____ baseball team named after the large mountain range found in this U.S. state	j. Pittsburgh Steelers

Although sports are played all over the world, culture affects the influence of some sports leisure activities of people in different cultures. This chapter explores aspects of sports and leisure in the United States that may or may not be similar to what you find in your own culture. You will also practice language skills, including:

- recognizing word forms by using prefixes and suffixes
- activating background knowledge prior to reading
- categorizing ideas from a reading
- understanding literal and figurative meanings of sports idioms
- using *play* and *go* appropriately
- participating in small group discussions by interrupting politely
- interviewing English speakers
- listening for organization clues of time in a lecture
- researching basic information online
- understanding expressions of cause and effect

Vocabulary Development

Vocabulary Guessing Strategies: Word Morphology

When you read something in English, there may be words that you do not understand. Because it takes time to look up these words in the dictionary, it will help you to learn some strategies for guessing the meaning of these words. One way to do this is to look at the **morphology** of the word, or parts of the word.

A word can consist of a **prefix,** a **base,** and a **suffix.** Not every word, however, will have a prefix and/or a suffix. A **prefix** is one or more syllables that can be added to the front of a word or base, while a **suffix** can be added to the end. Their function is to change the meaning of the word. Many prefixes and suffixes come from Latin or Greek.

Look at this word you used in Chapter 2:

COOPERATION
prefix   base   suffix

The meanings of the prefix, base, and suffix are:

co = with, together
operat(e) = to work, to be in action (verb base)
tion = noun suffix

Therefore, we can guess that the word *cooperation* is a noun that means the act of working together.

A. The chart lists some common prefixes, their meanings, and an example of a word with that prefix. Blank spaces appear in the Example column. Fill in the blanks with a word that you have learned in this text.

Prefix	Meaning	Example
a-	without, not	atypical
anti-	against	antisocial
auto-	self	autonomous
con-, com-, col-, co-	together, with	_____
de-	reverse, opposite	devalue
ethn-	race or people	_____
e-, ex-	out from	_____
inter-	between, among	_____
mis-	wrong	misunderstand
pre-	before	_____
re-	back, again	_____
self-	independent, by oneself	self-help
un-	not	_____

B. Underline the suffixes in these words. One has been done for you as an example.

superfic<u>ial</u>	anthropologist	behavior	awareness	cultural
favorably	generalize	institution	unacceptable	integrate
acquaintance	distinctive	collectively	ethnocentrism	chronology
relationship	judgment	directness	memorize	truthful

Now, write the suffixes that indicate if a word is a noun, verb, adjective, or adverb into their appropriate place in the chart. One has been done for you as an example.

Noun Suffixes	Verb Suffixes
Adjective Suffixes	**Adverb Suffixes**
-ial	

Using your charts on prefixes and suffixes, make a list of some words that you have learned so far in this textbook. Add to this list as you go through this chapter.

1. _____   5. _____

2. _____   6. _____

3. _____   7. _____

4. _____   8. _____

I. Popular Sports in the United States

A. These words appear in the first reading on pages 59–60. Based on what you have learned about suffixes and the context of the words, decide whether each is a **noun, verb, adjective,** or **adverb.**

	Noun	Verb	Adjective	Adverb
incredible				
1. *incredible* athlete				
2. *incredibly* popular				
annual				
3. *annual* salary				
4. published *annually*				
protect				
5. police *protection*				
6. *protective* uniform				
nation				
7. *national* organization				
8. *nationally* recognized				
contribution				
9. *contribute* to charity				
10. major *contributor*				
require				
11. certain *required* courses				
12. a daily *requirement*				
professional				
13. *professional* career				
14. played soccer *professionally*				

B. Before you read Leisure Time, write what you already know about the three most popular sports in the United States, and write questions about what you would like to know. Share your questions with a few classmates to see if you have similar questions and/or if they know any of the answers to your questions.

_____

`

_____

_____

Activating Background Knowledge before Reading

As you skim a text for the general idea, you should think about what you already know about the topic, and then ask yourself a few questions about what you would like to know. By doing this, you are moving toward a better understanding of the topic.

	What You Already Know?	**What You Would Like to Know?**
Baseball		
American football		
Basketball		

Leisure Time

The United States is such a large and diverse country that there are pastimes and leisure activities to suit everyone. Sports—for both spectators and participants— are a major part of most people's lives. Among the most popular of spectator sports are three that originated in the United States—baseball, American football, and basketball.

Baseball

Baseball, often called the national game by Americans, is not only very popular, but it has contributed many words and phrases that have become a part of the English language. For example, someone might say that a person who has attempted something and failed has **struck out.** A **ballpark figure** is an approximate number. A **pinch hitter** is someone who steps in for another person, often in an emergency. Doing something very well is hitting a **home run.**

A baseball field has three bases and **home,** called home plate. Each team fields nine players: three outfielders, a pitcher, a catcher, a first baseman, second baseman, third baseman, and shortstop. Many children play baseball either at school or in Little League, a national organization of baseball teams for children. Baseball is also played in colleges and universities. The best college players usually go on to play baseball professionally. There are several levels of professional baseball, but only the major leagues are nationally discussed and attended. Adults also play baseball or softball for fun, sometimes with colleagues from work, or against a team from other companies.

The major leagues include the American (features a designated hitter) and the National Leagues (the pitcher hits). The season lasts from April to October. The best teams in each league play against each other in playoffs and then the winners of each meet in the championship, or World Series.

Football

American football is not the game known as football in most other parts of the world. Originally, this game was similar to rugby football, which is where the name came from. It's played by two teams of eleven players; because one team stops the other by **tackling,** the players wear protective equipment that prevents injury. The field has two **endzones,** 100 yards apart. A team scores **touchdown** by getting in the other team's endzone.

Football is played by organized teams in schools, usually starting in junior high school and high school. College football is a popular spectator sport and a major source of **income** for colleges and universities, due to revenues from sponsorship deals with corporations and TV broadcasting. The college football season is active September through November, and it officially ends around New Year's Day with bowl games played by the best teams from around the country.

Professional football is played by the teams of the National Football League (NFL) in a season that runs from late summer to January. The championship game is called the Super Bowl. The Super Bowl is always one of the top—if not the top—rated TV shows every year.

Basketball

Basketball is perhaps the most exciting of all spectator sports. It is also a favorite leisure game for many people since it requires little equipment other than a ball and a net, called a **basket.** Five players from each team play against each other using different types of shots. The game is very fast-paced. Basketball courts are found in a many parks and public spaces. Basketball has become one of the biggest professional sports, with top players earning huge amounts of money both for playing and for promoting products such as sports shoes. (Other professional athletes earn large salaries too.)

The professional basketball organization is the National Basketball Association (NBA), which holds its annual championship, the World Championship (or NBA Finals), early each summer. College basketball is just as popular and gets just as much television coverage as professional games. The NCAA college basketball tournament (March Madness, or the Final Four) is played each spring.

C. Categorize the items from the reading by writing each one in the appropriate category. More than one category may be possible.

Final Four   Super Bowl   eleven players   World Series

April to October   Little League   New Year's Day   March Madness

ballpark   strike out   NBA   NFL

court   bowl games   pinch hitter   net

tackling   touchdown   home run   endzone

Baseball	Football	Basketball

Using *go* and *play* with Various Sports

Choosing the correct verb when talking about sports can sometimes be confusing. In general, use *go* with sports/activities that one usually does alone. Use *play* with sports that are competitive.

D. Fill in the blank with the correct form of *go* or *play*.

1. My parents usually _____ golf on weekends.

2. Will you _____ skiing when you go to the mountains this weekend?

3. John _____ racquetball with his boss every Friday morning before work.

4. I used to _____ bowling every Saturday night.

5. He learned how to _____ tennis when he was very young; last year he won four tournaments.

6. I love to _____ swimming in the ocean in the summer.

7. We plan to _____ hiking and then camp by the river overnight.

8. I plan to drive to a quiet lake in the mountains and _____ fishing.

9. Although it does not seem as popular as basketball and baseball, many children in the U.S. _____ soccer when they are young.

E. In Chapter 2, you learned about idioms related to the body. There are also several idioms related to sports, like this one from Leisure Time:

For example, someone might say that a person who has attempted something and failed has struck out.

What does to strike out mean in this sentence?

Understanding Figurative versus Literal Meaning

In baseball, to *strike out* means to swing the bat and not get a hit within the maximum number of times allowed (three). This is the **literal,** most basic meaning of the expression. But this expression has adopted a **figurative** meaning as well, which is "to try and fail at something." The figurative meaning is more abstract, such as, "The new president *struck out* with his health care plan."

Each of these words or expressions has both a literal and figurative meaning. Choose a figurative meaning from on the left and its literal meaning from the right. The first one has been done for you as an example.

Figurative Meanings	Word/Expression	Literal Meanings
1. to do something very well	_b_ huddle _c_	a. to get a hit (single, double, triple, or homerun) every time
2. to take someone by surprise (usually unpleasantly)	__ kick-off __	b. to stop playing a game for a certain amount of time to get advice from the coach, to rest, etc.
3. something that is certain to happen	__ slam dunk __	c. the gathering of a team to discuss the next play, to get directions from the coach, etc.
4. very important, well-known	__ to bat a thousand __	d. as a batter, to walk up and be ready to receive a pitch
5. the beginning of a project or event	__ to throw a curveball __	e. a very forceful, dramatic way to score a goal in basketball
6. to get together as a group to discuss something	__ to step up to the plate __	f. to pitch a ball that changes direction and is difficult to hit
7. to take a break	__ in the big leagues __	g. the start (or re-start) of play in a game
8. to get ready to do something	__ take a timeout __	h. part of a major, professional team (rather than a minor league)

Interrupting Politely

When you are participating in group discussions, there are usually one or two people who seem to dominate the conversation. In order to make sure that your opinions are heard, you may have to interrupt the speakers so that you can take the floor. Some polite expressions that you can use to do this are:

Excuse me/Pardon me. . . . I'd like to say something.
Can I add/say something here?
That reminds me of. . . .
May I interrupt for a second?

F. Discuss the questions with a small group of students. Practice interrupting each politely so that all members of your group participate equally.

1. Which is your favorite sport to play? Why?

2. Which is your favorite sport to watch on TV? Why?

3. Which is your favorite sport to watch in person (live)? Why?

4. Which sport do you think is the most dangerous? Why?

5. Do you have a favorite athlete? Who? Why?

6. Some of the highest paid basketball players in the U.S. earn $20,000,000 a year. Do you think this is fair? Why or why not?

7. Do you think athletes should be role models or considered heroes? Why or why not?

G. Find two or three Americans to interview about the three most popular sports in the United States and the world's most popular sport, soccer.

Part 1

Ask two Americans to finish these sentences. Take notes on their responses, and bring them to class.

	American #1	American #2
1. Baseball is. . . .		
2. Baseball players are. . . .		
3. Football is. . . .		
4. Football players are. . . .		
5. Basketball is. . . .		
6. Basketball players are. . . .		
7. Soccer is. . . .		
8. Soccer players are. . . .		

Part 2

In groups, share the responses you have from interviewing Americans. Some questions you may want to consider:

1. What are the similarities among your responses and the others in your group?

2. What are some of the differences among your responses and the others in your group?

3. Were any of the responses surprising to you? Why or why not?

II. History of Extreme Sports

 A. Listen to the introduction to the lecture, and answer the questions.

1. This lecture will be about which of the following?

   a. soccer in the U.S. and other countries

   b. the description and history of extreme sports

   c. reasons why people do not like traditional sports

2. What words did the speaker say that helped you answer this question?

_____

Understanding Lecture Organization

There are many language clues you can listen for that will help you understand the organization of a talk or lecture. Understanding the organization will help you make predictions about what the person will say and will also help you to remember information better because it is related to something.

Introductory Clues

Some lecturers state their goals very clearly such as, *Today I will talk about X,* or *I'd like to cover three goals.* Other speakers may not state their purpose very clearly. As a listener, you generally should not worry about taking notes during the introduction. Instead, listen carefully to see if you can understand the purpose and organization of the entire talk.

Chronological Clues

In the lecture on the history of extreme sports, several language clues are used to organize the lecture. The organizational pattern the lecturer uses is **chronology,** which provides the reader with a time frame. Some language clues a writer can use with this organizational pattern include *first, next, in 1998, two years later,* and other variations.

B. Read these sentences. Underline the expressions that indicate when these events took place.

1. At that time there were nine different categories.

2. Two years after the first Summer X Games, the first Winter X Games took place in California in 1997.

C. Listen to the full lecture the first time without taking any notes. Follow the timeline on the left with your finger and listen to the speaker move from one idea to the next. (Ignore Other Key Information for now.)

What Happened?	Other Key Information
1. ____ 1960s	a. ESPN changes name to X Games
2. ____ 1993	b. Summer X Games in San Diego
3. ____ 1995	c. ESPN talks about organizing extreme sports competition
4. ____ 1996	d. 1st international X Games in Thailand
5. ____ 1997	e. 1st Winter X Games
6. ____ April 1998	f. surfing is popular
7. ____ June 1998	g. Tony Hawk does first 900-degree spin in San Francisco
8. ____ 1999	h. 1st Latin X games in Brazil
9. ____ 2001	i. 1st Extreme Games in Rhode Island and Vermont
10. ____ November 2001	j. 1st public skate park opens in Atlanta
11. ____ February 2002	k. U.S. snowboarding team at Winter Olympics
12. ____ March 2002	l. 24-hour coverage of X Games
13. ____ 2006	m. ESPN hosts 1st Action Sports and Music Awards

 D. Listen to the lecture again. This time, take some notes that will help you match the year and events. Then go back to Activity C, and match the years and events.

E. The lecture concentrated on the history of extreme sports. Choose one of these sports/activities (or something else that you are interested in) that is popular in the United States, and fill in the chart below after you find information on the Internet. Summarize the information to the class.

tailgating	NASCAR	skateboarding
American football	March Madness	basketball
cheerleading	Rose Bowl	volleyball

Other: _____

Topic: _____

Description:

When did it start?

Where did it start?

Who started it?

Finding Information on the Internet

Doing searches on the Internet can be useful for finding basic answers to topics of popular interest. You can do a general search by typing *history of X* to find out the answers to questions in sports history: *what*, *when*, *where*, and *who*.

Although doing a general search can answer basic questions, be aware that there can be thousands of websites on a particular topic from many different types of sources. It's a good idea to compare information on several websites and to be aware of the source of the information, so that you read and use the most reliable and accurate information available.

III. Americans and Fitness

Walking for fitness, jogging, swimming, and weight-training are the most common activities that Americans do to stay in shape. Over the past several years, fitness classes in health clubs and recreation centers at universities have been added that include many other ways to keep in shape.

A. Scan the catalogue descriptions for classes offered at the Student Recreation Center at Georgia State University on page 71, and answer the questions.

1. Which fitness class is based on martial arts from Thailand?

2. Which dance class is based on traditional dances of North Africa and the Middle East?

3. Which class has both African and Brazilian influences?

4. Which fitness class includes training with weapons?

5. Which class includes current popular dances from Africa?

6. What is Bando?

Bando Kickboxing

Simple, powerful techniques form the extremely effective self-defense and fighting style (similar to Muay Thai) of Bando, the ancient martial system of Burma. This class offers training in martial arts forms, weapons, and animal styles, as well as light-medium, and some full-contact sparring.

Capoiera

This unique art originated as a fighting style based on rhythmic patterns. The intent was to disguise the martial art as dance. While Capoeira originated in Africa, the strong Brazilian influence forms the basis for this class.

Lotus Self-Defense

Lotus Self-Defense is a martial arts style from Thailand. We teach basic moves: punches, kicks, blocks, and rolls with an emphasis on practical self-defense. Lotus is a combination of Thai kick-boxing, Aikido, Judo, and Kenpo karate.

Belly Dance

Belly dance is composed of the traditional dances of North Africa and Middle East offering a low-impact mild cardiovascular workout based on upper and lower body isolations. Cultural music, costume, and dance styles will be reviewed during the class session.

Chinese Dance

This class offers you a fantastic opportunity to learn a variety of Chinese dances, including Tibet, Mongolian dance, and Chinese folk/ classic/belly dance. Different types of music, culture, and dance styles will be reviewed, and students will learn to dance with silk fans, ribbons, and Chinese minority costumes.

Nigerian Dance

Come explore the current popular dances from Africa and traditional dances from all parts of Nigeria. This class offers a mild cardiovascular workout by isolating your upper and lower body. African music, clothing, and dance styles will be reviewed during the class session.

B. Many visitors to the United States often notice that there are many overweight people. It is a fact that during the past 20 years there has been a dramatic increase in obesity in the United States. Read the article that explains why.

Currently, the United States is showing a trend of physical inactivity paired with increasing rates of obesity. Americans are becoming older and are more consumed by stress and concerns over money.

According to recent studies, the majority of Americans, about 55 percent, do not the get the recommended amount of exercise to promote good health. The Centers for Disease Control and Prevention (CDC) recommend 30 minutes of moderate exercise most days, or 20 minutes vigorous exercise three or more days a week.

In addition *The Journal of the American Medical Association* cites that nearly one-third of Americans are obese and roughly another third are overweight. The CDC reports that obesity is the fastest-growing health problem in the United States and is second only to smoking. About only half of 12- to 21-years-olds engage in regular, vigorous physical activity. As a result, childhood obesity rates have more than doubled since the early 1970s.

According to Mediamark Research's Teen Intelligence Report, teens are stressed because of their schoolwork, lack of sleep, and not having enough spending money. A 2004 Harris poll found that adults are stressed about the economy and their jobs.

Looking to the future, the first baby boomers (born between 1946–1965) turn 65 in 2010 and typically are reported to feel 12 years younger than their age, according to the Southeastern Institute of Research. This age group is active and wants programs that aid them in maintaining youthful spirit, mind and body.

Source: From Atilano, Daniel, "Tracking the Trends," *Parks & Recreation, 41,* no. 3 (March 2006).

Recognizing Signal Words of Cause and Effect

In the reading, there were some reasons given for the rise in obesity among teenagers and adults. Look at this sentence:

About only half of 12- to 21-year-olds engage in regular,
vigorous exercise. As a result, childhood obesity rates have
more than doubled since the early 1970s.

In this sentence, the writer shows cause and effect by using the expression, *As a result.*

Cause: Only half of 12- to 21-year-olds engage in regular, vigorous exercise.
Effect: Childhood obesity rates have more than doubled since the early 1970s

There are other words/expressions that can be used to show cause and effect:

because	as a result of	cause(s)	as a result
since	because of	lead(s) to	therefore
		contribute(s) to	consequently
		result(s) in	
		is/are more likely	

C. In the sentences that follow, identify the cause(s) and effect(s) using the signal words to help you.

1. *Teens are stressed because of their schoolwork, lack of sleep, and not having enough spending money.*

   Cause(s): _____

   Effect(s): _____

2. *Since obese people usually don't want other people to look at them when they are exercising, it becomes difficult to encourage them to join health clubs.*

   Cause(s): _____

   Effect(s): _____

3. *Younger people are more likely to be in better shape if they get interested in playing organized team sports like soccer.*

   Cause(s): _____

   Effect(s): _____

4. *Because people want to look and feel good, they are willing to try many different types of exercise to get into shape.*

   Cause(s): _____

   Effect(s): _____

5. *Regular exercise leads to improved overall health, physical appearance, and self-confidence.*

   Cause(s): _____

   Effect(s): _____

IV. Values Application

Read the headlines from the sports section of the newspaper. Which value(s) do you think each one reflects?

a. equality

b. progress

c. individualism

d. materialism

1. ____ **More youngsters choosing solo skateboarding over joining a baseball team**

2. ____ **Chicago's New Basketball Superstar Tops Highest Salary at $23,500,988**

3. ____ **New girls' football team added to meet state and federal fairness guidelines**

4. ____ **Local Health Club Installs High-Tech Video Games On Fitness Equipment**

CHAPTER 4

Hitting the Books:
The American Education System

A list of scrambled names of subjects taught in American schools appears on page 76. Can you figure out the subjects?

1. tgomyree	geometry
2. tasssciitt	statistics
3. glaerba	algebra
4. ogibloy	biology
5. rshiyto	history
6. hpicyss	physics
7. iscola esdusit	Social studies
8. ysphailc neodutaci	P.E
9. ramda	drama
10. ucocgaitnn	accounting
11. yphcyoolsg	psychology
12. suclualc	calculus

After you finish the chapter, return to this page and decide at which level of American education each of the subjects is usually taught.

In addition to learning about some aspects of the American philosophy of education, the organization of the American school system, American public school enrollment, American higher education, and important problems and issues in American public education, you will also practice:

- using an English-English dictionary
- participating in whole class situations by answering questions aloud
- recognizing and using pronoun reference words
- writing a persuasive formal letter
- using abbreviations and symbols in note-taking
- recognizing supporting details
- recognizing common abbreviations used in American university systems
- scanning schedules for specific information
- paraphrasing sentences

After completing this chapter, return to this page and assess your own achievement in reaching these objectives.

Vocabulary Development

A good English-English dictionary can tell you much more about a word than just the meaning. Each dictionary will probably use slightly different abbreviations and formats; however, this entry from *The American Heritage Dictionary of the English Language* should be consistent with most dictionaries. The specifics about your dictionary will be explained in the front pages.

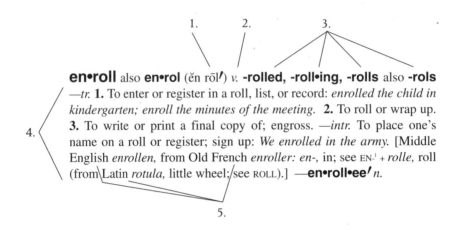

1.   2.   3.

en•roll also **en•rol** (ĕn rōl′) *v.* **-rolled, -roll•ing, -rolls** also **-rols**
—*tr.* **1.** To enter or register in a roll, list, or record: *enrolled the child in kindergarten; enroll the minutes of the meeting.* **2.** To roll or wrap up. **3.** To write or print a final copy of; engross. —*intr.* To place one's name on a roll or register; sign up: *We enrolled in the army.* [Middle English *enrollen*, from Old French *enroller: en-*, in; see EN-¹ + *rolle*, roll (from Latin *rotula*, little wheel; see ROLL).] —**en•roll•ee′** *n.*

4.

5.

A. Put the number from the dictionary entry on the line next to its corresponding explanation.

_____ Etymology (history of the word)

_____ Part of speech (verb, noun, adjective, etc.)

_____ Meaning(s) of the word

_____ Inflected forms (how the word changes from its base form to indicate different parts of speech)

_____ Syllabification, pronunciation

B. Now look at the entire page of entries from the same dictionary. Scan it quickly for answers to the questions.

1. How many syllables does the word *entangle* have? What symbol does this dictionary use to separate the syllables?

2. Where is the stress in the word *enrichment*? What symbol is used to show where the stress is?

3. What part of speech is the word *enshrine*? What is the alternate spelling?

4. How many different undefined forms are provided for the word *enslave*?

5. From what three languages did the word *ensign* come?

6. For certain words, many dictionaries also provide synonyms (different words that have a similar meaning). What is a synonym for the word *ensue*?

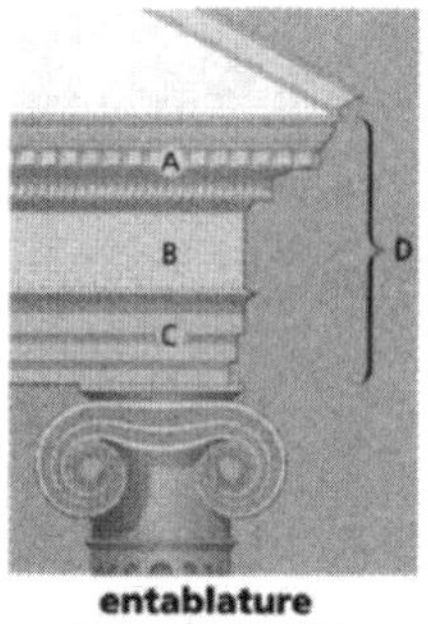

entablature
an Ionic order entablature
A. cornice
B. frieze
C. architrave
D. entablature

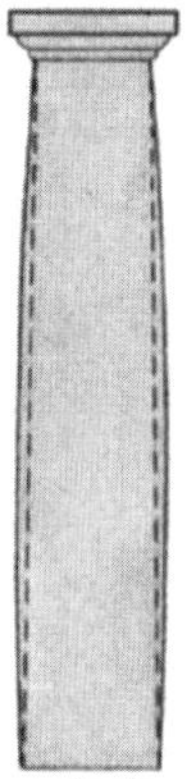

entasis

ă pat, ā pay, âr care, ä father, ĕ pet, ē be, ĭ pit, ī pie, îr pier, ŏ pot, ō toe, ô paw, oi boy, ou out, ŏŏ took, ōō boot, ŭ cut, ûr urge, th thin, *th* this, hw which, zh vision, ə about, item, ♦ regionalism

Stress marks: **ʹ** (primary); ʹ (secondary), as in **dictionary** (dĭkʹshə-nĕrʹē)

en•rapt (ĕn-răptʹ) *adj.* Filled with delight; enraptured.

en•rap•ture (ĕn-răpʹchər) *tr.v.* **-tured, -tur•ing, -tures** To fill with rapture or delight. **—en•rapʹture•ment** *n.*

Synonyms *enrapture, entrance, ravish, thrill, transport* These verbs mean to have a powerful, agreeable, and often overwhelming emotional effect on someone: *enraptured by the music; scenery that entranced us; a painting that ravished the eye; thrilled by their success; transported with joy.*

---

en•rich (ĕn-rĭchʹ) *tr.v.* **-riched, -rich•ing, -rich•es 1.** To make rich or richer. **2.** To make fuller, more meaningful, or more rewarding: *An appreciation of art will enrich your life.* **3.** To add fertilizer to. **4.** To add nutrients to: *The dairy enriched its milk with vitamin D.* **5.** To add to the beauty or character of; adorn: *"Glittering tears enriched her eyes"* (Arnold Bennett). **6.** *Physics* To increase the amount of one or more radioactive isotopes in (a material, especially a nuclear fuel). [Middle English *enrichen,* from Old French *enrichier* : *en-,* causative pref.; see EN–¹ + *riche,* rich; see RICH.] **—en•richʹer** *n.*

en•rich•ment (ĕn-rĭchʹmənt) *n.* **1.** The act of enriching or the state of being enriched. **2.** Something that enriches.

en•robe (ĕn-rōbʹ) *tr.v.* **-robed, -rob•ing, -robes** To dress in or as if in a robe.

en•roll also **en•rol** (ĕn-rōlʹ) *v.* **-rolled, -roll•ing, -rolls** also **-rols** *—tr.* **1.** To enter or register in a roll, list, or record: *enrolled the child in kindergarten; enroll the minutes of the meeting.* **2.** To roll or wrap up. **3.** To write or print a final copy of; engross. *—intr.* To place one's name on a roll or register; sign up: *We enrolled in the army.* [Middle English *enrollen,* from Old French *enroller* : *en-,* in; see EN–¹ + *rolle,* roll (from Latin *rotula,* little wheel; see ROLL).] **—en•roll•eeʹ** *n.*

en•roll•ment also **en•rol•ment** (ĕn-rōlʹmənt) *n.* **1a.** The act or process of enrolling. **b.** The state of being enrolled. **2.** The number enrolled: *The class has an enrollment of 27 students.* **3.** A record or an entry.

en•root (ĕn-rōōtʹ, -rŏŏtʹ) *tr.v.* **-root•ed, -root•ing, -roots** To establish firmly by or as if by roots; implant.

en route (ŏn rōōtʹ, ĕn) *adv. & adj.* On or along the way: *We are en route to the museum. The store is en route.* [French : *en,* on + *route,* route.]

ENS or **Ens.** *abbr.* ensign

en•san•guine (ĕn-săngʹgwĭn) *tr.v.* **-guined, -guin•ing, -guines** To cover or stain with or as if with blood.

En•sche•de also **En•sche•da** (ĕnʹskə-dāʹ, -SKHə-) A city of eastern Netherlands near the German border. It is a textile center. Population: 147,486.

en•sconce (ĕn-skŏnsʹ) *tr.v.* **-sconced, -sconc•ing, -sconc•es 1.** To settle (oneself) securely or comfortably: *She ensconced herself in an armchair.* **2.** To place or conceal in a secure place. [EN–¹ + SCONCE¹.]

en•sem•ble (ŏn-sŏmʹbəl) *n.* **1.** A unit or group of complementary parts that contribute to a single effect, especially: **a.** A coordinated outfit or costume. **b.** A coordinated set of furniture. **c.** A group of musicians, singers, dancers, or actors who perform together: *an improvisational theater ensemble; a woodwind ensemble.* **2.** *Music* **a.** A work for two or more vocalists or instrumentalists. **b.** The performance of such a work. [French, from Old French, together, from Late Latin *īnsimul,* at the same time : *in-,* intensive pref.; see IN–² + *simul,* at the same time; see **sem-¹** in Appendix I.]

En•se•na•da (ĕnʹsə-näʹdə) A city of northwest Mexico on the Pacific Ocean. It is a popular resort. Population: 120,483.

en•serf (ĕn-sûrfʹ) *tr.v.* **-serfed, -serf•ing, -serfs** To make into or as if into a serf.

en•sheathe (ĕn-shē*th*ʹ) *tr.v.* **-sheathed, -sheath•ing, -sheathes** To cover or enclose with or as with a sheathe.

en•shrine (ĕn-shrīnʹ) also **in•shrine** (ĭn-) *tr.v.* **-shrined, -shrin•ing, -shrines 1.** To enclose in or as if in a shrine. **2.** To cherish as sacred. **—en•shrineʹment** *n.*

en•shroud (ĕn-shroudʹ) *tr.v.* **-shroud•ed, -shroud•ing, -shrouds** To cover with or as if with a shroud: *Fog enshrouded us.*

en•si•form (ĕnʹsə-fôrmʹ) *adj.* Shaped like a sword, as the leaf of an iris. [Latin *ēnsis,* sword + –FORM.]

en•sign (ĕnʹsən, -sīnʹ) *n.* **1.** A national flag displayed on ships and aircraft, often with the special insignia of a branch or unit of the armed forces. **2.** A standard or banner, as of a military unit. **3.** *Archaic* A standard-bearer. **4.** (ĕnʹsən) *Abbr.* **ENS a.** A commissioned rank in the U.S. Navy or Coast Guard that is below lieutenant junior grade. **b.** One who holds this rank. **5a.** A badge of office or power; an emblem: *"I want the seals of power and place,/The ensigns of command,/Charged by the people's unbought grace,/To rule my native land"* (John Quincy Adams). **b.** A sign; a token. [Middle English *ensigne,* from Old French *enseigne,* from Latin *īnsignia,* insignia. See INSIGNIA.]

en•si•lage (ĕnʹsə-lĭj) *n.* **1.** The process of storing and fermenting green fodder in a silo. **2.** Fodder preserved in a silo; silage. ❖ *tr.v.* **-laged, -lag•ing, -lag•es** To ensile. [French, from *ensiler,* to ensile. See ENSILE.]

en•sile (ĕn-sīlʹ) *tr.v.* **-siled, -sil•ing, -siles** To store (fodder) in a silo for preservation. [French *ensiler,* from Spanish *ensilar* : *en-,* in (from Latin *in-);* see EN–¹ + *silo,* silo.]

en•slave (ĕn-slāvʹ) *tr.v.* **-slaved, -slav•ing, -slaves** To make into or as if into a slave. **—en•slaveʹment** *n.* **—en•slavʹer** *n.*

en•snare (ĕn-snârʹ) also **in•snare** (ĭn-) *tr.v.* **-snared, -snar•ing, -snares** To take or catch in or as if in a snare. See synonyms at **catch. —en•snareʹment** *n.* **—en•snarʹer** *n.*

en•snarl (ĕn-snärlʹ) *tr.v.* **-snarled, -snarl•ing, -snarls** To entangle in or as if in a snarl: *"The Senate has contrived to ensnarl several major proposals in two legislative tangles"* (New York Times).

En•sor (ĕnʹsôr), **James** 1860–1949. Belgian painter whose works, such as *Entry of Christ into Brussels* (1888), influenced surrealism and often feature nightmarish, masked faces.

en•sor•cell or **en•sor•cel** (ĕn-sôrʹsəl) *tr.v.* **-celled, -cel•ling, -cells** or **-celed, -cel•ing, -cels** To enchant; bewitch. [French *ensorceler,* from Old French *ensorcerer, ensorceler* : *en-,* intensive pref.; see EN–¹ + *sorcier,* sorcerer; see SORCERER.] **—en•sorʹcell•ment** *n.*

en•soul (ĕn-sōlʹ) also **in•soul** (ĭn-) *tr.v.* **-souled, -soul•ing, -souls 1.** To endow with a soul. **2.** To place, receive, or cherish in the soul.

en•sphere (ĕn-sfîrʹ) also **in•sphere** (ĭn-) *tr.v.* **-sphered, -spher•ing, -spheres** To enclose in or as if in a sphere.

en•sta•tite (ĕnʹstə-tītʹ) *n.* A glassy, usually yellowish gray variety of orthorhombic pyroxene having a magnesium silicate base, mainly $MgSiO_3$, usually found embedded in igneous rocks and meteorites. [Greek *enstatēs,* adversary (because of its refractory quality) : *en-,* in, at, near; see EN–² + *-statēs,* one that stands; see **stā-** in Appendix I + –ITE¹.]

en•sue (ĕn-sōōʹ) *intr.v.* **-sued, -su•ing, -sues 1.** To follow as a consequence or result. See synonyms at **follow. 2.** To take place subsequently. [Middle English *ensuen,* from Old French *ensuivre, ensu-,* from Vulgar Latin **īnsequere,* from Latin *īnsequī,* to follow closely : *in-,* intensive pref.; see EN–¹ + *sequī,* to follow; see **sekʷ-¹** in Appendix I.]

en suite (äN swētʹ) *adv. & adj.* In or as part of a series or set: *a room and its furniture that were decorated en suite; en suite decorations.* [French : *en,* in + *suite,* a following, sequence.]

en•sure (ĕn-shŏŏrʹ) *tr.v.* **-sured, -sur•ing, -sures** To make sure or certain; insure: *Our precautions ensured our safety.* See Usage Note at **assure.** [Middle English *ensuren,* from Anglo-Norman *enseurer* : Old French *en-,* causative pref.; see EN–¹ + Old French *seur,* secure, variant of *sur;* see SURE.]

ENT *abbr. Medicine* ear, nose, and throat

ent– *pref.* Variant of **ento–.**

–ent *suff.* **1a.** Performing, promoting, or causing a specified action: *absorbent.* **b.** Being in a specified state or condition: *bivalent.* **2.** One that performs, promotes, or causes a specified action: *referent.* [Middle English, from Old French, from Latin *-ēns, -ent-,* present participle suff.]

en•tab•la•ture (ĕn-tăbʹlə-chŏŏrʹ) *n.* The upper section of a classical building, resting on the columns and constituting the architrave, frieze, and cornice. [Obsolete French, from Italian *intavolatura,* from *intavolare,* to put on a table : *in-,* in, on (from Latin; see EN–¹) + *tavola,* table (from Latin *tabula,* board).]

en•ta•ble•ment (ĕn-tāʹbəl-mənt) *n.* A platform above the base and the dado of a pedestal. [French, from Old French : *en-,* in, on; see EN–¹ + *table,* table; see TABLE + *-ment,* -ment.]

en•tail (ĕn-tālʹ, ĭn-) *tr.v.* **-tailed, -tail•ing, -tails 1.** To have, impose, or require as a necessary accompaniment or consequence: *The investment entailed a high risk. The proposition* X is a rose *entails the proposition* X is a flower *because all roses are flowers.* **2.** To limit the inheritance of (property) to a specified succession of heirs. **3.** To bestow or impose on a person or a specified succession of heirs. ❖ *n.* **1a.** The act of entailing, especially property. **b.** The state of being entailed. **2.** An entailed estate. **3.** A predetermined order of succession, as to an estate or to an office. **4.** Something transmitted as if by unalterable inheritance. [Middle English *entaillen,* to limit inheritance to specific heirs : *en-,* intensive pref.; see EN–¹ + *taille,* tail; see TAIL².] **—en•tailʹment** *n.*

en•ta•moe•ba (ĕnʹtə-mēʹbə) also **en•da•moe•ba** (ĕnʹdə-) *n., pl.* **-bas** or **-bae** (-bē) Any of several parasitic amoebas of the genus *Entamoeba,* especially *E. histolytica,* causing dysentery and ulceration of the colon and liver. [New Latin *Entamoeba,* genus name : ENT(O)– + AMOEBA.]

en•tan•gle (ĕn-tăngʹgəl) *tr.v.* **-gled, -gling, -gles 1.** To twist together or entwine into a confusing mass; snarl. **2.** To complicate; confuse. **3.** To involve in or as if in a tangle. See synonyms at **catch. —en•tanʹgle•ment** *n.* **—en•tanʹgler** *n.*

en•ta•sis (ĕnʹtə-sĭs) *n., pl.* **-ses** (-sēzʹ) A slight convexity or swelling, as in the shaft of a column, intended to compensate for the illusion of concavity resulting from straight sides. [Latin, from Greek, tension, from *enteinein,* to stretch tight : *en-,* intensive pref.; see EN–² + *teinein,* to stretch; see **ten-** in Appendix I.]

En•teb•be (ĕn-tĕbʹə, -tĕbʹē) A town of southern Uganda on Lake Victoria. Formerly (1894–1962) the capital of Uganda, it is the site of an international airport, where in 1976 Israeli commandos rescued hostages held aboard a plane by Palestinian hijackers. Population: 41,638.

en•tel•e•chy (ĕn-tĕlʹĭ-kē) *n., pl.* **-chies 1.** In the philosophy of Aristotle, the condition of a thing whose essence is fully realized; actuality. **2.** In some philosophical systems, a vital force that directs an organism toward self-fulfillment. [Late Latin *entelechīa,* from Greek *entelekheia* : *entelēs,* complete (*en-,* in; see EN–² + *telos,* completion; see **kʷel-¹** in Appendix I) + *ekhein,* to have; see **segh-** in Appendix I.]

en•tente (ŏn-tŏntʹ) *n.* **1.** An agreement between two or more governments or powers for cooperative action or policy: *"the economic entente between the Soviet Union and western Europe"* (Robert W. Tucker). **2.** The parties to such an agreement. [French, from Old French, intent, from feminine past participle of *entendre,* to understand, intend. See INTEND.]

en•ter (ĕnʹtər) *v.* **-tered, -ter•ing, -ters** *—tr.* **1.** To come or go into: *The train entered the tunnel.* **2.** To penetrate; pierce: *The bullet entered the victim's skull.* **3.** To introduce; insert: *She entered the probe into the patient's artery.* **4a.** To become a participant, member, or part of; join: *too old to enter the army; entered the discussion at a crucial moment.* **b.** To gain admission to (a school, for example). **5.** To cause to become a participant, member, or part of; enroll: *entered the children in private school; entered dahlias in a flower show.* **6.** To embark on; begin: *With*

C. Use your dictionary to look up any words you don't understand in this chapter. Keep a list of these words and study them often.

I. Philosophy of American Education

Some basic principles and ideals on which the American education system has evolved are listed. These principles have been established by several educational philosophers throughout the years.

1. All Americans should have equal access to public education.

2. The educational system should strive to produce high school students who are 100 percent literate.

3. The federal government does not have control over schools; schools are governed by local school districts.

A. Match each statement about American education listed below with one of the three principles shown in this chart.

Equal access to education	Strive for 100% literacy among high school students	Local, not national control

a. Standardized examinations should NOT prohibit further study after high school.

b. Individual states determine the curriculum.

c. Physically and mentally challenged students are admitted in colleges/universities.

d. Students must attend school until age 16 (in most states).

e. Community colleges allow for less academically able students to earn a degree.

f. Courses are provided to non-native speakers of English to prepare them for American colleges and universities.

g. Public schools are funded by property taxes in the districts in which they are located.

h. More than 85 percent of Americans complete at least four years of high school or more.

i. State and local governments have a lot of control over schools.

B. Summarize the educational philosophy of your country. What similarities are there between the United States and your country? Differences?

_____

_____

_____

_____

II. The Organization of American Schools

A. Let's now look at the structure of schools. How many hours a day did you go to elementary school? Junior high school or middle school? High school? What subjects did you study? Compare your answers with other students in your class.

B. Read the passage.

Structure of American Schools

The American school system includes public, private, and parochial schools. Public schools are funded through state and local taxes; students at private schools, in contrast, usually have to pay tuition to attend the school, and they often are required to wear uniforms. Although the administration of private and public schools is different, and many schools are experimenting with different programs, the structure of many schools is relatively the same.

Compulsory education in the United States begins around age 6. Children can quit school around age 16 in more than half of the states, but most states discourage this by requiring parental permission. In addition, it is very difficult to get a job in the United States without a high school diploma or the G.E.D. (general equivalency diploma).

The first year of required education in most elementary school systems is kindergarten. The rules vary among states, but in general, children are approximately the same age (5–6) when they begin kindergarten. Some parents choose to send their children to nursery school (preschool) prior to kindergarten, but this is not required. Children are introduced to a social environment and learn basic skills of coordination in nursery school. In kindergarten, children go to school for half a day (either morning or afternoon), and, in addition to learning how to interact socially, they begin some preliminary work in basic skills, such as reading and writing.

Elementary school usually includes grades 1–5 or 1–6. Grades 6–8 (or 7–9) are often housed in a different building than the lower grades. These schools are called either middle schools or junior high schools. Students in elementary schools (also called grade schools or grammar schools) usually meet with the same teacher in the same room during the day. Basic subjects such as math, social studies, science, and sometimes art and music are covered.

Between the ages of 12 and 14, American students attend junior high school or middle school. This period is usually considered part of American secondary education. Junior high school students take certain compulsory courses that are included in the curriculum of that state. For the most part, these courses include English, general math, physical education, general science, and social studies. Students can also take elective courses such as foreign language, vocational arts, or consumer science.

High school usually begins with either 9th or 10th grade. Its curriculum can include either college preparatory or vocational courses, depending on the interests of the student. College prep courses include English, math, science, and foreign languages. Vocational courses include technical or trade subjects, such as automobile mechanics, woodworking, or drafting. Students at all levels (freshman, sophomore, junior, senior) are also able to choose several elective courses.

Extracurricular activities (student council, sports, band, choir, language clubs, etc.) are very popular among some high school students. Participation in extracurricular activities is considered an important part of the socialization of the students. The purpose of the activities is to help students develop interests outside of their academic courses and to help develop a feeling of "school spirit." The clubs usually support themselves by raising money through fund-raising activities.

The school year for most states in the United States lasts from mid-August or early September until May or June. It may be longer in some states, depending on the length of vacations and the number of required school days. Some schools divide the year into quarters (three sessions) and others use the semester system (two sessions). Classes are held Monday through Friday with a variation on hours between 7:30 and 3:30. Students involved in extracurricular activities often stay after school for meetings or sports practice.

Even though there may be some variation in the structure of elementary, junior high, and high schools in the United States, most states follow the above-mentioned pattern. There are several experimental schools, however, that are addressing the problems in American education and have started to break with many of the traditions.

Participating in Class

In American college courses, especially those that require a lot of outside text-book reading, students are often expected to show that they have read the material by answering questions that the instructor directs to the whole class, so you need to understand questions that your instructor delivers *orally*.

To be prepared, you should, of course, read the material. Also, during the first couple of weeks of classes, you should try to understand the "culture" of the classroom. In other words, is it okay to simply say the answer aloud? Should you raise your hand first?

 C. Listen to your teacher call on students to answer questions about the reading. Make notes as you hear the questions and answers. Share your responses with a classmate.

1.

2.

3.

4.

5.

6.

D. Recognizing the relationship between words in a text increases comprehension. Look at this sentence from the reading:

> The school year for most states in the United States lasts from mid-August or early September until May or June. It may be longer in some states, depending on the length of vacations and the number of required school days.

What does *It* refer to?

Using Pronoun Reference Words

An author will often make use of references, words, or phrases that refer to a previous (and sometimes following) idea in the text. This technique is used to avoid unnecessary repetition in his or her writing. A key skill for English learners is to recognize these reference words and determine the words or ideas they refer to. The first step is to be aware of the different referencing techniques the author uses. One technique is pronoun reference.

Use pronouns to indicate the previously stated noun or noun phrase.
  a. Subject and object pronouns:

> Junior high schools are very similar to high schools. Students are allowed to take some elective courses, and *they* also change rooms and teachers throughout the day.

  b. Possessive pronouns:

> Several American high school students are very busy with *their* part-time jobs and extracurricular activities.

  c. Demonstrative pronouns *(this/that, these, those, others, such)*:

> The students call their English professor by her first name. *This* informality is common among some American university professors.

E. Read these sentences. Identify the words or phrases that the italicized words refer to.

Example: Some schools divide the year into quarters (three sessions) and *others* use the semester
system (two sessions).

others ⇒ schools

1. In kindergarten, children go to school for half a day (either morning or afternoon), and, in
addition to learning how to interact socially, *they* also begin some preliminary work in basic
skills such as reading and writing.

they ⇒_____

2. Between the ages of 12 and 14, American students attend junior high school or middle school.
This period is usually considered part of American secondary education.

This period ⇒_____

3. Junior high school students take certain compulsory courses that are included in the curriculum of that state. For the most part, *these* include English, general math, physical education,
general science, and social studies.

these ⇒_____

4. Prior to kindergarten, some parents choose to send their children to nursery school (pre-
school), but *this* is not required.

this ⇒_____

5. High school usually begins with either 9th or 10th grade. *Its* curriculum can include either college preparatory or vocational courses, depending on the interests of the student.

Its ⇒_____

6. Compulsory education in the United States begins around age 6. Children can quit school
around age 16 in more than half of the states, but most states discourage *this* by requiring
parental permission.

this ⇒_____

F. Electives, which are courses chosen by the students, are popular in most American high schools. Categorize the different electives, and then discuss the questions on page 89 with a small group.

French	woodworking	gymnastics	automobile repair
dance	school newspaper	drama	German
radio broadcasting	orchestra	Spanish	tennis
basketball	~~carpentry~~	sculpture	photography
web design	creative writing	American sign language	choir

performing arts	
visual arts	
vocational education	*carpentry*
physical education	
foreign languages	
journalism/publishing	

1. Do you think offering students electives is a good idea in middle school/junior high school and high school? Why or why not?

2. Do you think electives help prepare students for college? Why or why not?

3. Did you take any elective courses in high school? Why or why not? If you did, what were the topics of your courses?

4. Do you have any ideas for other types of electives?

G. In the United States, some high school students get part-time jobs while they are in high school. There are, of course, several advantages and disadvantages to students working while in high school. Which of the following are advantages (A) to working students and which are disadvantages (D)?

1. _____ Students learn how to work hard to earn money.

2. _____ Students might get hurt at their part-time jobs.

3. _____ Students may be tired during their classes.

4. _____ Students might not always finish their homework.

5. _____ Students may spend less time with their friends.

6. _____ Students can start saving money for college.

7. _____ Students learn responsibility and gain experience for a future career.

8. _____ Students can learn to become more independent.

H. In groups, imagine that you are members of the student council (student government). You have been asked by other students to help convince parents and teachers that students should be able to choose whether to have a part-time job. Review the advantages in Activity G, and provide several examples for each.

I. Using the format provided, write a letter to Diane Sherwood, the school principal of Wilkins High School, and persuade her to support students' decisions to work part-time during the school year.

September 16, 2———

Principal Diane Sherwood
Wilkins High School
1651 Touhy Ave.
Justice, IL 60973

Sincerely,

III. Enrollment in American Schools

 A. Listen to the sentence that comes from a lecture about enrollment in American schools. What do you think your notes should look like: *a* or *b*?

   a. "The number of 3 to 5 year-olds enrolled in nursery school increased from 27.1 percent in 1965 to 63.9 percent in 2001."

   b. # of 3–5 yr. olds enrolled in school ↑ from 27.1% in '65 to 63.9% in '01

Using Abbreviations and Symbols in Note-Taking

There are many situations you may find yourself in where you want to take notes (academic lecture, business meeting, etc.). The challenge in taking notes is to (1) try to understand the organization of the talk in order to organize your notes; (2) identify the important details; and (3) write fast enough to record these details. This is a difficult job in a first language and a more difficult job in a second language. Therefore, it is important to be patient and understand that note-taking is a skill that requires a lot of practice.

To help you take notes more quickly, you can use several note-taking symbols and abbreviations. There are no "rules" for how to abbreviate words, or make them shorter. People all use symbols and abbreviate words a little differently, but there are some guidelines that you should keep in mind:

1. Use standard symbols (see the exercise that follows).
2. Shorten dates (September 2, 2007 → 9/2/07).
3. Use the first syllable and/or first few letters of the second (history → hist.).
4. Omit vowels (develop → dvlp.).
5. Omit prepositions and articles (*a, of, the, on,* . . .).
6. After first use, abbreviate proper nouns (Scholastic Aptitude Test → SAT).

B. Match the note-taking symbols on the left with their meaning. Write the appropriate letter in the blank.

1. ___ =   a. therefore
2. ___ <   b. approximately
3. ___ >   c. increase
4. ___ &   d. for example
5. ___ w/   e. without
6. ___ ↑   f. less than
7. ___ →   g. with
8. ___ e.g.   h. equals, is
9. ___ ↓   i. more than
10. ___ ≅   j. number
11. ___ ∴   k. decrease
12. ___ #   l. between
13. ___ w/o   m. cause
14. ___ ~   n. and

C. Rewrite the sentences using abbreviations and note-taking symbols.

Example: Enrollment in public elementary and secondary schools rose 22 percent between 1985 and 2005.

Elem. & second. school enroll. ↑ by 22% ~ '85 & '05.

1. Between 2003 and 2016, the number of high school graduates is projected to increase nationally by 6 percent.

_____

_____

2. The cost of tuition for public four-year universities increased from an average of $1,318 in 1985 to $5,836 20 years later in 2006. This is less than private universities, which charged approximately $22,218 for tuition and fees in 2006. This does not include room and board for either public or private universities, which can average from approximately $6,900 to nearly $8,100 a year.

_____

_____

_____

3. The sources of money for public schools vary among the states. For example, in the state of Georgia, 43.7 percent of the money for schools comes from the local school districts and 48.2 percent comes from state taxes. The rest of the money comes from federal and private sources. In New Mexico, however, 12.9 percent comes from the local districts and 72 percent of the money comes from the state, with the rest coming from federal and private sources.

_____

_____

_____

D. Listen to the entire lecture. Take notes here using note-taking symbols and abbreviations.

E. Listen to the lecture again, and answer the questions using your lecture notes.

1. T / F   There are approximately 43 million students in American public schools.

2. T / F   About 65,000 American students attend private schools.

3. T / F   The United States has more than 50,000 school districts.

4. T / F   New Jersey spends more money per student than any other state.

IV. American Higher Education

A. In groups, brainstorm what you know about American colleges and universities. Think about these questions.

1. How many colleges and universities do you think there are in the U.S.? 1,000? 2,000? 4,000?

2. What are the different degrees one can earn at American colleges and universities?

3. What do you think the average tuition is?

4. Why do you think residents of a different state or country pay more than residents for a state school?

B. Use these words in the sentences.

affiliation	interchanged	plentiful	prior
funded	obtain	postsecondary	

1. Universities and colleges are _____ in large urban areas in most American cities.

2. Private and religious institutions can be very expensive because they do not receive the same type of funding that public schools do, although they may _____ some money from the state for certain programs.

3. _____ to attending the first year at a university, students usually participate in an orientation session.

4. Some private schools have religious _____ (Protestant, Roman Catholic, and Jewish), but it is usually not necessary to be a member of that particular religion to attend the school.

5. The words *college* and *university* are often _____, but it is generally understood that a university offers graduate degrees as well as undergraduate degrees.

6. _____ education includes any education one obtains after high school, including community college courses.

7. Public universities are owned and _____ by the states in which they are located.

C. Read the article about higher education. Ignore the blank lines in the article for now. You will work with these in Activity E.

Higher Education in the United States

The higher education system in the United States is one of the largest in the world._4_ _1_ This broad range of choices in postsecondary education provides every student with an opportunity to attain his or her personal and occupational goals. Universities are plentiful in large urban areas in every American city. However, if a person prefers a more rural setting, there are also hundreds of colleges located away from the large cities.

Higher education in the United States includes any program of study at two-year colleges, four-year colleges and universities, and graduate schools._____

_____ The words *college* and *university* are often interchanged, but it is generally understood that a university can offer graduate degrees as well. These degrees can be quite specialized, such as a Master of Arts in a particular subject or even doctorate degrees.

American colleges and universities may be public, private, or religious. Public universities are owned and funded by the states in which they are located. Students pay tuition at public universities, but those who have resided in the state for a certain period of time prior to beginning classes do not pay as much as nonresidents. _____ These costs, however, depend on the size, location, reputation, etc. of the university.

Private and religious institutions can be very expensive because they do not receive the same type of funding that public schools do, although they may obtain some money from the state for certain programs. Some American private universities are considered the best in the nation, if not in the world, but the costs of these schools are very high._____ Some private schools have religious affiliations (Protestant, Roman Catholic, and Jewish), but it is usually not necessary to be a member of that particular religion to attend the school. In fact, some of the affiliations are purely historical.

Last, there are also some technical institutions that are privately owned, like businesses._7_ The training is very specialized, and the goals of the student are specifically related to a particular occupation.

D. Of these two sentences about American higher education, which is more convincing?

1. The average cost of a four-year college is expensive. It increases each year.

2. The average cost of a four-year college is expensive. Each year, it increases as much as 12–15 percent at some institutions.

> ### Recognizing Supporting Details
>
> You already know that most writing in English is organized from general to specific. In a paragraph, the most general statement is usually the **topic sentence.** The topic sentence is followed by specific statements, which are called **supporting details.** Supporting details are very important for writing because they help the reader understand your main point more easily, and they convince the reader about the point you are making. Supporting details can usually be categorized into one or more of the following:
>
> - facts or statistics
> - examples
> - personal experiences
> - observations
> - statements by authorities

E. These statements are all specific details about higher education in the United States. Review the reading. Every place there is a blank line, a supporting detail(s) is needed. Write the number(s) of the sentences on the correct line(s) in the reading. If there is one line, choose one of the sentences. If there are two lines, choose two supporting details.

1. Students can choose among large research institutions with more than 25,000 students or smaller colleges with fewer than 1,000 students.

2. A nonresident student may pay as much as 50 or 60 percent more than a resident student.

3. The average cost of tuition, fees, and room and board at private four-year colleges was $30,367 in 2006–7.

4. There are more than 4,100 community colleges, colleges, and universities in the United States.

5. Two-year colleges, often called community colleges, offer the Associate of Arts or the Associate of Science degrees (A.A. or A.S.).

6. Four-year colleges grant undergraduate bachelor's degrees (B.A. or B.S.).

7. These technical institutes offer two-year programs in such fields as automotive engineering, business, and electronics.

F. Answer these questions about the reading on page 96.

1. Why do you think private colleges and universities are more expensive than public ones?

_____

_____

2. What degrees do junior colleges offer? Four-year colleges?

_____

_____

3. What is the difference between a college and a university? Do you think that both words are used to describe postsecondary education?

_____

_____

4. Why do you think that tuition for nonresidents is more expensive at public schools?

_____

_____

5. Would you rather attend a large public university or a small private university? Why?

_____

_____

G. Many abbreviations and initials are used in American universities. Try to guess what each abbreviation from college campuses represents, and then write each abbreviation in the appropriate column. One example has been done for you.

Courses	Degrees	Grades/Exams
econ. = economics		

A.A.   GMAT   Ph.D.   econ.   bio.

A.S.   prereq.   poli. sci.   GPA   SAT

ACT   psych.   M.A.   P.E.   B.S.

H. Scan the course schedule that follows in order to answer the questions.

1. What class is offered at 4:00 on Mondays, Wednesdays, and Fridays?

2. Which course is the only one available for a student who has to take night classes?

3. Which course does Professor Larsson teach?

4. Which three courses have multiple sections?

5. Who teaches the honor section of Anthropology 100?

6. When does Anthropology 340 meet?

7. How many minutes does each Tuesday/Thursday class last?

Call #	Subject	Course	Credit	Title	Days	Time	Instructor	Location	Comments
11972	ANTH	100	3	Human Origins	MWF	9:00 AM–9:50 AM	McGowan	MH 120	
*****	ANTH	100	3	Human Origins	MWF	9:00 AM–9:50 AM	Meeks	AH 340	This section for honor students only; you must obtain call number from the Lee Honors College (MH 352)
12544	ANTH	110	3	Lost Worlds/ Archaeology	TR	1:00 PM–2:15 PM	Bray	AH 340	
12543	ANTH	110	3	Lost Worlds/ Archaeology	TR	11:00 AM–12:15 PM	Bray	SH 420	
12364	ANTH	120	3	Peoples of the World	MWF	1:00 PM–1:50 PM	Ketza	ALC 43	
12697	ANTH	120	3	Peoples of the World	TR	9:30 AM–10:45 AM	Flood	AH 340	
12587	ANTH	120	3	Peoples of the World	W	1:00 PM–3:30 PM	Meeks	MH 120	
15498	ANTH	120	3	Peoples of the World	MWF	2:00 PM–2:50 PM	Gobron	GCB 675	
*****	ANTH	120	3	Peoples of the World	TR	8:00 AM–9:15 AM	Bunting	ALC 43	This section for Freshman Learning Community only; you must obtain call number for FLC office (GCB 130)
16457	ANTH	130	3	Human Evolution	MWF	8:00 AM–8:50 AM	Snell	GCB 675	
13256	ANTH	210	3	Intro to Archaeology	TR	11:00 AM–12:15 PM	Nelson	MH 120	
17853	ANTH	240	3	Environmental Archaeology	MWF	4:00 PM–4:50 PM	Scheller	ALC 43	
16872	ANTH	330	3	Cultures of Africa	T	6:30 PM–9:00 PM	Kountz	MH 120	
13648	ANTH	340	3	Cultures of Mid East	TR	9:30 AM–10:45 AM	Hutton	GCB 675	
19834	ANTH	380	3	Principles of Cult Anth	TR	1:00 PM–2:15 PM	Light	SH 420	
16579	ANTH	392	3	Anthropology in Action	MWF	1:00 PM–1:50 PM	Larsson	SH 420	

MH=Moore Hall
AH=Arts & Humanities
SH=Sparks Hall
ALC=Anderson Learning Center
GCB=General Classroom Building

V. Problems in American Education

A. Before we learn about a few problems facing American education, brainstorm some possible problems that you think are common to educational systems in countries all over the world.

B. Former Presidents George H. W. Bush and Bill Clinton proposed and signed into legislation several goals in the mid-1990s that were referred to as the Goals 2000. This was one of those goals:

> *Every school will promote partnerships that will increase parental involvement and participation in promoting the social, emotional, and academic growth of children.*

Now read another version of the same goal. Does this version say the same thing? How is this version different?

> *All schools will encourage relationships that help parents become more involved and participate in their children's social, emotional, and academic growth.*

Paraphrasing

Paraphrasing is a process by which writers express someone else's meaning in their own words. Paraphrasing is a very helpful tool when you are trying to remember new concepts or vocabulary that are difficult; it is much easier to remember them if you can say them in your own words!

Paraphrasing other people's words and ideas is a very difficult skill. You must not only understand the meaning, but you must also rewrite the language yet keep its original meaning. Paraphrasing requires a great deal of practice and skill.

How to Paraphrase

Read the passage very carefully to make sure you understand the meaning. Put the material aside and then write in your own words what you remember. Check your writing against the original by rereading the passage to make sure that you have

      a. conveyed the same meaning;

      b. kept your paraphrase about the same length; and

      c. written the paraphrase in your own style of writing.

Techniques for Paraphrasing

1. Change the grammatical structure:

      a. join short sentences or break up long ones

      b. change the active verbs to passive or the passive verbs to active

      c. change the word order

2. Change the vocabulary to more common synonyms/expressions and simpler phrases. However, you should not change technical vocabulary (global economy), proper names, (former President George H. W. Bush), or numbers/statistics (90 percent, 2000).

C. Read some of the other Goals 2000. Then, paraphrase them in your own words.

1. The high school graduation rate will increase to at least 90 percent.

   _____

   _____

   _____

2. American students will be first in the world in mathematics and science achievement.

   _____

   _____

   _____

3. Every school in the United States will be free of drugs, violence, and the unauthorized presence of firearms and alcohol and will offer a disciplined environment conducive to learning.

   _____

   _____

   _____

4. The nation's teaching force will have access to programs for the continued improvement of their professional skills and the opportunity to acquire the knowledge and skills needed to instruct and prepare all American students for the next century.

   _____

   _____

   _____

D. As was mentioned in the beginning of the chapter, many of the goals in education are often ideals—it is very difficult, if not impossible, for the educational systems across the country to meet all of these goals. Look at the list of problems that follows regarding the American education system. Which of the Goals 2000 (1–4) in Activity C is each problem related to?

1. Goal # _____: In 1998–99 academic year, 3,523 students were expelled for bringing a firearm to school. This is a decrease from the 5,724 students expelled in 1996-97 for bringing a firearm to school.

2. Goal # _____: The percentage of secondary school teachers who hold a degree in their main teaching assignment has decreased.

3. Goal # _____: The percentage of students who report that someone offered them drugs at school has increased.

4. Goal # _____: In 2003, over four-fifths (85 percent) of all adults 25 years or older reported they had completed at least high school.

5. Goal # _____: Results of the Third International Mathematics and Science Study (TIMSS) involving a half-million students in 41 countries indicate that by 4th grade, American students only score in the middle of 26 countries reported and by 8th grade, they are in the bottom third.

E. In small groups, choose one of the problems/goals matching from Activity D and brainstorm possible ways to improve the situation or solve this problem.

VI. Values Application

A. Read the letter that an international student wrote to her friend describing her first year of high school as an exchange student in the United States. Ignore the numbers for now.

Dear Brea,

Hi! How are you? I just finished my first semester here. So far, my junior year abroad in the United States has been fantastic! I have made a lot of new friends, and I'm really glad that I decided to spend a year here, although I am surprised at the differences between the schools here and the ones at home.

The first day I walked into the high school, I was shocked. I knew I probably wouldn't have to wear a uniform, but when my math teacher walked into the room wearing jeans and gym shoes, I couldn't believe it! (1).

Another big difference is that I was able to choose all my courses. Of course, we all have to take some science, math, and English courses, but since I really like biology more than chemistry, I signed up for microbiology (2). I did really well on my last exam in that class. When the teacher returned them, I noticed that nobody in the class showed each other their scores. I guess students like to keep their grades to themselves here (3).

A lot of students in my math class are seniors, so they're starting to look at colleges for next year. Many of them are working part-time now to save money for college (4). Most of them do not know what they want to major in, but the counselors here have encouraged them to wait and specialize during their second or third year of college. Many of them took tests called the ACT and the SAT last month. Compared to our country, it seems that anyone can go to almost any college he or she wants because here the students don't have to pass an entrance exam (5). In fact, my host brother, who has had a difficult time in high school and has not received very good grades, will be able to attend community college by taking some special courses during his first year (6).

I hope you're enjoying school too. I miss you very much, and I'm looking forward to seeing you next June.

Your friend,

Jina

B. Reread the numbered sentences in the letter and decide which value from Chapter 1 is reflected in each statement.

1. _____

2. _____

3. _____

4. _____

5. _____

6. _____

CHAPTER 5

Earning a Living:
The American Workplace

Source: iStockphoto.com.

Read these statements about working in the United States. Do any of these statements or statistics surprise you?

1. Each year, Americans lose 574 million vacation days because they do not use them.

2. Maternity leave at most companies is three months and is often unpaid; paternity leave is unusual.

3. Thirty percent of employees do office work during vacation.

4. Forty five percent of U.S. workers did not use all of their vacation time due to them in 2006.

5. Among 16 European countries—Australia, Canada, Japan, New Zealand, and the United States—the United States is the only country in the group that does not require employers to provide paid leave.

6. Can you match each weekly average salary in the right-hand column of the chart with the occupation?

Occupation	Average Weekly Earnings
1. _____ Elementary and middle school teachers	a. $332
2. _____ Lawyers	b. $352
3. _____ Carpenters	c. $556
4. _____ Computer programmers	d. $824
5. _____ Child care workers	e. $826
6. _____ Police officers	f. $935
7. _____ Physicians/surgeons	g. $1,086
8. _____ Waiters	h. $1,366
9. _____ Registered nurses	i. $1,547
10. _____ Aircraft pilots	j. $1,609

Source: U.S. Department of Labor, Bureau of Labor Statistics, 2005.

In this chapter we will look at the American workplace and further study the American values that are present in everyday living. Some aspects of the workplace will be discussed, including different types of occupations, sexist and nonsexist job titles, and the earnings and benefits of several different occupations. As with the other chapters, significant American values in the workplace will also be explored. You will practice language skills including:

- recognizing and using different word forms
- scanning a reading and newspaper article for specific information
- filling in an outline of a reading
- avoiding sexist language
- predicting syllable stress
- participating in a group discussion
- interpreting information on a graph
- recognizing synonyms

Vocabulary Development

In Chapter 3, we learned about suffixes, which can indicate the different parts of speech, such as nouns, verbs, adjectives, and adverbs. In the dictionary, these forms are often listed and undefined at the end of the definition. The chart that follows lists some of the vocabulary words you will encounter in this chapter. Complete the chart. Remember that the word form may not be the same for all the words and that some boxes will be empty.

Noun	Verb	Adjective	Adverb
	classify		——
employer, employee			——
			collaboratively
		industrialized	——
		qualified	——
	cooperate		
	——		efficiently
benefit			
		managerial	——
		required	——
			administratively
	achieve		——
		evaluated	——

I. Different Types of Occupations in the United States

In industrialized societies, there are a wide variety of occupations. Occupations can be classified in several different ways, but many American jobs are categorized and referred to based on the amount of skill or training that is necessary to perform the job, as well as where the work is performed.

A. Scan the reading passage, and list the four different categories of occupations.

1. _____

2. _____

3. _____

4. _____

B. Read the passage.

American Occupations: Past and Present

During the early colonization of the United States, most people were farmers. As the society became more industrialized, the number of necessary farmers decreased, and many people moved to larger, more urban areas of the country to find jobs. Because of new technology and industrialization, different types of occupations were developed.

With the shift from farming to industrialization, many blue-collar jobs were created. The U.S. Department of Labor reports that blue-collar jobs make up about 23 percent of the workforce. Blue-collar jobs typically require some kind of manual labor and can be divided into three different types: unskilled, semi-skilled, and skilled labor. Unskilled jobs require little formal education; most of the necessary skills can be learned directly on the job. Examples of unskilled blue-collar jobs include washing dishes and cooking at a fast food restaurant. Semi-skilled blue-collar workers often operate machines on assembly lines in large factories. These workers have received specific training for a specific skill such as automobile or electronic equipment assembly line work. Finally, skilled blue-collar work requires intense training in a specific trade. Most workers go through a training period, or apprenticeship. Plumbers, electricians, and other craftsworkers are all skilled workers who usually belong to unions that help protect them and regulate their work.

Just as industrialization created more blue-collar jobs, industrial technology created white-collar occupations. White-collar jobs now make up about 60 percent of the occupations in the United States as a result of the broad range of training, skills, and working environments that are involved. There are essentially two types of white-collar occupations. The first type concerns jobs that are based on the handling (producing, recording, classifying, and storing) of information. This type of white-collar occupation includes clerical (office), sales, managerial, administrative, or technical work. The second type includes the professionals, such as lawyers, doctors, teachers, and engineers, who usually have more specialized education backgrounds.

The third category of occupations is the fastest-growing sector in the economy—service jobs. Service occupations are replacing many of the manufacturing jobs that have disappeared as a result of advanced technology. Service workers, who make up about 14 percent of the labor force, provide some kind of service directly to individuals. Restaurant and hotel jobs, firefighting, and hair styling are some of the more obvious service occupations. In addition, many small businesses and organizations in the United States provide services such as cleaning (janitorial) and repairing of various products. There are also many Americans who work privately in many different types of service jobs, such as home health care aides, music teachers, etc.

Last, although it is the smallest sector of American jobs, farming occupations still exist. Not quite 3 percent of American workers are employed in agriculture as farmers, farm managers, or farm laborers. This category also includes occupations in forestry, fishing, and mining.

Although classifying jobs in this manner is helpful when describing the different sectors of the American workforce, labels like blue-collar, white-collar, service, and farm can be limiting because individuals may possess skills that cross categories. Also, job requirements change as new technology is developed.

References

- *Economics Today and Tomorrow.* Mission Hills, CA: Glencoe/McGraw Hill, 1991.
- U.S. Bureau of Labor Statistics. *Employment and Earnings.* Washington, DC: U.S. Department of Labor, 1995.
- Rose, P., P. Glazer, and M. Glazer. *Sociology: Understanding Society.* Englewood Cliffs, NJ: Prentice Hall, 1990.
- Current Statistics on White Collar Employees, 2003 Edition, Department of Professional Employees, AFL-CIO, Washington, DC.
- *http://www.bls.gov/opub/rtaw/pdf/intro.pdf*

C. Sometimes readers make outlines of a reading passage to understand it better. Fill in the missing parts in the outline on page 115 for this passage on job classifications. Some of the outline has already been filled in for you.

Outlining

Outlines are visual tools that represent the relationship and importance of ideas. Outlines are useful when listening to a lecture or when taking notes on a reading. Look at the format of the accompanying blank diagram of an outline. When you write an outline, remember these guidelines if your instructor asks you to turn one in:

1. Place ideas of equal importance at corresponding levels. For example, all the main ideas of an outline should go under the roman numerals (I, II, III), the next important ideas should go under the capital letters (A, B, C), etc.

2. Move from the very general at the first level (roman numerals) to the more specific as you progress down the levels (capital letters, ordinal numbers, etc.). In other words, the items listed next to a capital letter or an ordinal number are the supporting details for the main idea listed next to the roman numeral.

I. Industrialization of the United States
    A. More industrialization led to the decrease in farmers
    B. People moved to urban areas and different occupations were developed
II. Blue-collar workers (23% of the workforce)
    A. Unskilled labor
        1. dishwashers
        2.
    B.
        1. assembly line workers (automobile)
        2. assembly line workers (electronic equipment)
    C. Skilled labor
        1.
        2.
        3. other craftsworkers
III.
    A. Information handlers
        1. sales workers
        2.
        3.
        4.
    B.
        1. lawyers
        2. doctors
        3.
        4.
IV. Service workers (14% of the workforce)
    A. Major service organizations
        1. restaurant
        2.
        3.
        4.
    B. Small businesses/organizations
        1.
        2. repairing
    C.
        1. home health-care aides
        2. music teachers
V. Farmers (Not quite 3% of the workforce)
    A.
    B.
    C.
    D.

D. Categorize the different occupations into the appropriate categories in the chart that follows. In order to figure out which occupation fits into each category, ask yourself how much training or skill is necessary to perform the job, how long it takes to acquire the skill, and where the job is performed. Some examples are given.

supermarket cashier	professor	karate teacher	fire fighter
bus driver	beekeeper	computer programmer	office manager
machinist	accountant	plastic surgeon	nurse
physical therapist	home health aide	executive assistant	bodyguard

White-Collar	Blue-Collar	Service	Farm
physician	truck driver	police officer	farmer

Avoiding Sexist Language

When writing or talking about occupations, effort should be made to avoid sexist language. In other words, assumptions should not be made that a particular job is a "man's job" or a "woman's job." Use generic job titles that do not indicate gender. For example, currently the word *actor* is being used to refer to both male and female actors.

E. Some sexist job titles appear on the left. Can you unscramble the letters of the words in the right column to reveal the nonsexist alternatives?

Sexist Job Titles	Nonsexist Job Titles
1. sound man	nsoud necthiiacn <u>sound technician</u>
2. handyman	pshydanoner _____
3. fireman	reif gfireht _____
4. workman	rokwre _____
5. chairman	pciesrharon _____
6. mailman	aplost rrrciae _____
7. stewardess	glithf tatenatnd _____
8. policeman	lpioce fifcroe _____
9. businessman	pbussseinenors _____

F. Look at the list of subjects and occupations. Based on the number of syllables and the stress (see Chapter 2), put the words in the appropriate place in the chart. One has been done for you as an example.

~~economics~~   politics   history   psychologist

engineer   politician   ~~economist~~   psychology

historian   mathematician   engineering   mathematics

Subject	Person
1. OO●O economics	O●OO economist
2. O●OO	O●OO
3. OO●O	OO●
4. ●OO	O●OO
5. ●OO	OO●O
6. OO●O	OO●O

G. Discuss these questions about working in small groups. Are your answers similar to others in your group?

1. When you were a child, what did you want to be when you grew up? Has your idea changed? Why or why not?

2. Which jobs are considered the most prestigious in your culture? Why?

3. Which jobs are considered the least prestigious? Why?

4. What kind of job would you never do?

5. If money were not a problem, what would your "dream job" be?

6. If you had to choose between a satisfying job or a well-paid one, which would you choose? Why?

7. Do you think men and women should get paid the same for the same job?

H. In July 2006, approximately 500 Americans were asked by the Harris Poll to evaluate the prestige (status) of several different occupations. Put a 1 in front of the occupation you consider to be the "most prestigious" and a 10 by the occupation you consider to be to the "least prestigious." Your instructor will tell you how Americans rated these.

1. _____ police officer

2. _____ actor

3. _____ teacher

4. _____ athlete

5. _____ farmer

6. _____ firefighter

7. _____ journalist

8. _____ lawyer

9. _____ accountant

10. _____ doctor

I. Individually or in groups, list one occupation for each letter of the alphabet.

A = architects	B =	C =	D =
E =	F =	G =	H =
I =	J =	K =	L =
M =	N =	O =	P =
Q =	R =	S =	T =
U =	V =	W =	X =
Y =	Z =		

II. Earnings and Benefits

A. In groups, brainstorm the benefits (in addition to money) that the different people might get in each occupation.

Occupation	Possible Benefits
clothing store clerk	free or discounted store merchandise
college professor	
high school teacher	
flight attendant	
restaurant manager	
book publisher	

B. Read the passage.

Earnings and Benefits for American Jobs

The earnings and benefits a worker receives in the United States vary according to several factors. In the United States, a person's earnings are based on different types of pay plans. Workers may be paid an annual salary (paid weekly, bimonthly, or monthly), an hourly wage, commissions based on a percentage of what they sell, or an amount for each item they produce. Others receive tips for services to customers. Workers also may be paid a combination of a salary plus commission or a salary or hourly wage plus bonus or tips.

Benefits can vary depending on where an employee works. Most state and local government employees, for example, generally have better medical and dental care, life insurance, retirement plans, and different options for time off than workers in the private sector.

Many workers receive employer-paid benefits in addition to wages and salaries. These are informally called *perks* (short for perquisites). Teachers, for example, get summers off; college faculty get sabbatical leave and tuition for dependents; pilots, flight attendants, and aircraft mechanics working for airlines get free or discounted air travel for themselves and their families; and retail sales workers get discounted merchandise.

Benefits can also vary with the size of the company. Workers employed in medium and large firms with 100 or more employees enjoy better benefits than workers in small firms with fewer than 100 workers. Medium and large firms generally provide better medical and dental insurance, life insurance, and retirement benefits, as well as longer unpaid maternity leave and long-term disability insurance. Unlike in most developed countries, maternity and paternity leave in the United States is often unpaid. Paid vacations and holidays and medical care and life insurance are generally the major benefits available to the majority of workers in small firms.

Finally, benefits vary depending on whether the work is full time or part time. For example, only 36 percent of part-time employees receive paid vacations and holidays, compared to 90 percent of full-time workers. Most Americans do not enjoy very long vacations, however. Two weeks per year is the average length of vacation for most Americans, but the length of the vacation certainly depends on the length of employment. Most American employees have to work for a company longer than 10 years in order to receive more than two to three weeks of vacation.

In conclusion, earnings and benefits depend on where a person works, the size of the company, and whether or not the person works part time or full time.

References

- U.S. Bureau of Labor Statistics. *Occupational Outlook Handbook. Bulletin 2450.* Washington, DC: GPO, 1995.
- Biracree, Tom, and Nancy Bicaree. *Almanac of the American People.* New York: Facts on File, 1988, 161.
- Ray, Rebecca, and John Schmitt. *No-Vacation Nation.* Washington, DC: Center for Economic and Policy Research, 2007.

C. Read the following statements. Write a T if the sentence is true or an F if the sentence is false.

1. _____ Employees of small firms usually have better benefits than those of larger firms.

2. _____ Most Americans have to work for a company for a year in order to get more than two or three weeks vacation.

3. _____ Retirement benefits are usually available to employees of medium and large companies.

4. _____ Maternity and paternity leave in the United States are always paid.

5. _____ Part-time employees usually receive benefits similar to those of full-time employees.

D. Some of these words are taken from the reading above. Three of the words on each line are similar in meaning. Circle the word that does not belong. Then, explain why each circled word does not belong.

1. wages	salary	job	earnings
2. worker	employee	employer	laborer
3. vacation	leave	holiday	overtime
4. cheaper	discounted	expensive	reduced
5. instructors	professors	clerical staff	faculty
6. benefits	perks	advantages	payments

E. Look at the graph and answer the questions that follow.

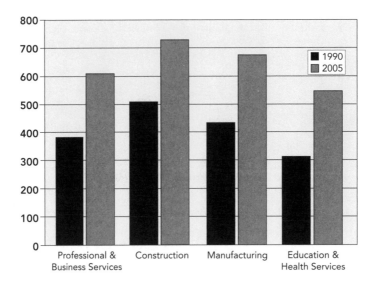

1. What is the subject of the graph?

2. What does the horizontal axis represent?

3. What does the vertical axis represent?

4. What conclusions can you draw from the graph?

Interpreting Graphs

Many textbooks and readings use graphs to show patterns over a period of time. Writers use graphs to help readers fully understand information. Line and bar graphs are the most common types of graphs in American textbooks. These graphs usually show data that concerns two variables, one on a vertical line, the other along a horizontal line. Information is indicated either by dots connected with a line (line graph) or with solid bars (bar graph). It is important to understand the information in the graph, and it is also important to be able to explain that information. Following are some useful expressions to use:

This graph shows . . . .
The subject of this graph is . . . .
The horizontal axis represents . . . .
The vertical axis represents . . . .
The pattern revealed by this graph is . . . .

F. Using the information regarding the history of the federal minimum wage rate in the United States, draw a bar graph. Do not forget to label your graph.

Year	Minimum Hourly Wage
1950	$0.75
1960	$1.00
1970	$1.60
1980	$3.10
1990	$3.80
2000	$5.15
2010*	$7.25

Source: Data from United States Department of Labor, Employment Standards Administration Wage and Hour Division, *http://www.dol.gov/esa/minwage/chart.htm.* July 24, 2007.

G. Scan the job postings, and list the names of the jobs in the appropriate place in the chart that follows.

800 General Help Wanted

Child care (afternoon only). Hickory Hills area. 3 girls: 6, 8, and 11. 20 hrs/wk., M–F. $12.00/hr.

Butterworth Healthcare
Home Health Aides

Up to $15/hr.
—Flexible hours
—Excellent wages/benefits
Call 555-9876

Service Tech for A/C and Heating. Apply at Champs Heating & Air Conditioning. Great wages and benefits. 64 W. Kalamazoo Ave.

Mount Prospect Public Schools
Hiring Bus Drives for Fall!
• paid training
• excellent salary, paid holidays, sick time, bonus, benefits
• off summers, winter and spring breaks
• must have good driving record

Mount Prospect Public Schools is an Equal Opportunity / Affirmative Action Employer

Pizza Delivery Person needed Fri. and Sat. nights only. Must have own car. $6.00/hr. + tips. Free pizza.

Restaurant Manager
New Market Expansion!
We're seeking experienced managers for upscale Chicago and Atlanta locations.
• attractive salaries
• excellent benefits
• promotion opportunities
• 5-day work week

Teacher's aide for Wilkins Junior High school 7th grade program. Mornings only. $8.75/hr., M, W, F only. Come to the administrative office between 10–2 on Friday, 8/4.

Jobs Paying an Hourly Wage	Jobs Paying a Salary	Jobs with Benefits (type of benefit, if specified)
Home health aide		

III. How Americans Work

A. This list of words and phrases comes from the newspaper article on page 125. Which are associated with cooperation, and which are associated with competition? Write them in the appropriate column of the chart that follows.

Cooperation	Competition

teamwork   individualism   self-centered

sharing information   capture the limelight   soloist

leading man or woman   collaboration   "me" culture

what is this going to do for me?   *I* must be replaced with *we*   trust

B. Before reading the newspaper article carefully, preview the article by looking at the title, subtitles, pictures, and picture captions. Write down any words or phrases in the space that follows that represent what the text will be about.

Making teamwork work

Angelo Henderson
From the *Detroit News,* September 5, 1994.

To promote teamwork, a Milford-based manufacturing firm launched a classroom program to teach employees how to listen and communicate better.

After five months of hearing plant workers grumble *"what is this going to do for me?"* the classes at A.B. Hello Inc. were canceled.

"What I couldn't understand was how they could sit at home the night before watching the best team win a game on TV, and then wonder why they needed to be a team at work," said Peter Rosenkrands, president of Heller, which produces diesel-injection systems:

Quickly, Rosenkrands learned that it takes more than classes to change the way employees think about teamwork—especially when American culture praises individualism.

"In this country, we are really motivated toward individual achievement and individual excellence," said Marietta Baba, professor of anthropology at Wayne State University.

And it's that self-centered mentality among American employees that's making it harder for U.S. companies to implement new ideas, develop more efficient processes and apply better technology to compete globally, she said. Baba speaks with authority. For the last five years, she has studied how cultural barriers hinder change in the workplace.

One result was "The Cultural Dimension of Technology-Enabled Corporate Transformation," a report compiled by Baba; Donald Falkenburg, professor and chairman of industrial and manufacturing engineering at Wayne State University; and David Hill, a former chief information officer of General Motors Corp.

The study was based on more than 500 interviews at all levels of operations in various automotive and aerospace companies undergoing new projects and programs.

The research added proof to the notion that what people think often is influenced by what they have experienced. And in America, the axiom is "Look out for No. 1."

From kindergarten through college, students are discouraged from sharing information or ideas—that's often considered cheating.

Typically, children are taught to find out what they do well, excel and compete against their peers, and be No. 1.

Often, it is one high achiever who captures the limelight, gaining more recognition than the entire group that made the task possible.

In a choir, it's the soloist. In a movie, it's the leading man or woman. In the operating room, it's the surgeon.

Likewise, in the corporate ranks, an employee is usually reviewed and evaluated individually, just like a cake in a bake-off at the state fair.

"We think competition among individuals brings out the best in people, but is also keeps people from cooperating," Baba said.

And that "me" culture in companies becomes *"my department, "my group," "my division,"* she said,

"In the traditional organization, the creative people develop a design and throw it over the walls to the engineers, who will do development and testing and throw it over the walls to the manufacturing people," Baba said.

"Problems are created when work groups don't cooperate. It's a much more expensive process because problems aren't detected early; work has to go back, and it becomes time consuming. A lot of quality problems can become about, resulting in higher costs."

The message is clear: cooperation, collaboration and trust. "I" must be replaced by "We."

C. Circle the correct synonym for the italicized word from the article in each sentence.

1. The research added proof to the *notion* that what people think often is influenced by what they have experienced.

    a. idea   b. desire   c. process

2. *Likewise*, in the corporate ranks, an employee is usually reviewed and evaluated individually.

    a. however   b. similarly   c. on the other hand

3. And it's that self-centered mentality among American employees that's making it harder for U.S. companies to *implement* new ideas.

    a. apply   b. ignore   c. create

4. It's a much more expensive process because problems aren't *detected* early.

    a. lost   b. solved   c. noticed

5. To *promote* teamwork, a Milford-based manufacturing firm launched a classroom program to teach employees how to listen and communicate better

    a. encourage   b. advertise   c. decrease

D. Answer the questions based on the newspaper article.

1. Why are students generally discouraged from sharing information or ideas in American schools?

2. According to Marietta Baba, what are negative aspects of competition?

3. What problems are created when work groups do not cooperate?

4. What has the American self-centered attitude made it harder for companies to do?

E. What are some ways that cooperation in the American workplace could be improved? Get into groups and decide what some effective ways might be to improve cooperation in the American workplace.

F. Just as the idea of competition and cooperation might differ between Americans and other cultures, the different perceptions of time are also an issue. In small groups, look at each of the different appointments listed in the chart that follows. Discuss what time you would arrive for each one in your country and then decide as a group what time an American would probably arrive. Are there differences between you and other people in your group or you and Americans? How are these times different and why?

Appointments	You	American
1. 1:00 PM job interview at a bank.		
2. 12:30 PM business lunch date.		
3. 7:00 PM dinner date with your boyfriend or girlfriend at a restaurant.		
4. Consecutive meetings at 1:00 PM and 2:00 PM.		
5. 8:00 AM business meeting.		
6. 9:00 PM party at a colleague's home.		

IV. Values Application

A. Read these statements. Which one do you think is fact and which is an opinion?

1. It's easy to get a job in the health care system in the United States.

2. The service-producing industry is the fastest growing industry in the United States.

Distinguishing between Fact and Opinion

Whenever you are reading, especially when you are reading about a controversial issue, it is important that you are able to distinguish between statements of fact and statements of opinion.

Facts are statements that can be proven true or false with evidence that is unbiased (someone's personal opinion).

Opinions can also be valid statements, even based on experience or research, but they usually express a personal point of view. Opinions cannot be proven with unbiased evidence.

It's not always easy to differentiate between a fact and an opinion because some statements present statistics to make them appear like facts, although a personal point of view is still expressed.

B. Read the statements regarding trends in the job market at the end of the century. Mark O for any statement you believe is an opinion or interpretation of the facts. Mark F for any statement you believe is a fact. Mark I for any statement you think is impossible to judge.

1. _____ Half-hour lunches in the United States are too short.

2. _____ Women are much more cooperative workers than men.

3. _____ According to a survey by DayTimers Inc., specialists in time management, the average American worker spends six hours per week working at home on job-related material.

4. _____ The number of women in the workforce has increased 44 percent since 1960.

5. _____ The American view of competition versus cooperation will lead to a failure in the U.S. economy.

6. _____ The average paid lunch hour in the United States is 27 minutes.

7. _____ The number of Americans who are self-employed continues to rise.

C. Look at the sentences in Activity B that describe several aspects of the American workplace. What values (see Chapter 1) do you think are reflected in each sentence?

CHAPTER 6

Getting Along

Family Life in the United States

What types of families do these pictures represent? Which ones do you think are the most common in the United States? Do you have friends/family in each type of family organization?

This chapter looks closely at the American family—its structure, the changes in this structure and the effects of these changes, American homes, the older generation, and the values associated with American family life. You will also practice language skills, including:

- creating vocabulary note cards
- participating in discussion
- writing a descriptive paragraph using signal words
- skimming longer texts for main ideas
- evaluating credibility of readings
- reviewing vocabulary strategies
- listening for arguments and counterarguments
- debating controversial issues
- writing persuasive essays
- maintaining and reviewing lecture notes

After completing this chapter, return to this page and assess your own achievement in reaching these objectives.

Vocabulary Development

Throughout this textbook, we have learned about syllable stress and morphology of words in English. In addition, we have learned certain strategies for guessing the meaning of words we don't know by looking at the word's morphology and the surrounding context. We have also studied how to use a dictionary to discover more about the pronunciation, grammar, and meanings of vocabulary words.

What is the best way to remember all of these new words? Researchers in second language acquisition believe that people will remember vocabulary better if it is presented in meaningful contexts and if it is recycled, or reused, again and again. All of the vocabulary that you learned in this text was important for understanding the larger picture of culture, and many of the important words were recycled throughout the chapters. This method of presentation should help you retain the new words that you learned in this book, but you will also probably need to do some extra studying of any new vocabulary words. Making and studying vocabulary cards are useful tools to help you remember words. Look at this example of a vocabulary card.

> norm(n): standard example of behavior; that which is regarded as average or acceptable
>
> normal (adj); normalize (v); normally (adv)
>
> Dual-career families have become the *norm* rather than the exception.

You do not need to follow the format of this card exactly; write out the information in a way that is helpful to you. Study these vocabulary cards whenever you have free time: riding on the train, eating dinner, waiting for an appointment or your next class to start, or just before you go to sleep.

I. Traditional Family Structures

A. Many families in the United States are considered **nuclear** families. The general definition of a nuclear family is one in which the mother, father, and children live in one house. **Extended** families, on the other hand, usually consist of grandparents, aunts, uncles, or cousins living in one house. Listen to these people describe their families. Decide whether each person comes from a nuclear family or an extended family. Write N for nuclear and E for extended.

1. _____

2. _____

3. _____

Now write some of the characteristics that you heard about nuclear families and extended families. You do not need to write complete sentences.

Nuclear Families	Extended Families

B. In small groups, discuss the advantages and disadvantages of living in either nuclear or extended families. Are there members in your group from each type of family?

	Advantages	Disadvantages
Nuclear families		
Extended families		

C. Choose either *nuclear* or *extended* families, and write one paragraph describing the advantages and disadvantage using ideas from your group discussion and signal phrases for descriptive paragraphs given in the box that follows.

Using Transition Signal Phrases in Descriptive Paragraphs

When you write different types of paragraphs, it is important to use signal words to help your readers move from one idea to the next easily. Use some of these phrases in your descriptive paragraph about nuclear *or* extended families:

One advantage . . .	*One disadvantage . . .*
Another advantage . . .	*An additional disadvantage . . .*
The most important advantage . . .	*A final disadvantage . . .*
The last advantage . . .	*The most significant disadvantage . . .*

These phrases highlight that there is a relationship among the sentences and helps your readers anticipate connected ideas.

II. Changing Family Structures

A. Read the quote, and answer the questions that follow.

"American families have always shown remarkable resiliency, or flexible adjustment to natural, economic, and social challenges. Their strengths resemble the elasticity[1] of a spider web, a gull's skillful flow with the wind, the regenerating[2] power of perennial[3] grasses, the cooperation of an ant colony, and the persistence of a stream carving canyon rocks. These are not the strengths of fixed monuments but living organisms. This resilience is not measured by wealth, muscle or efficiency but by creativity, unity, and hope. Cultivating[4] these family strengths is critical to a thriving human community."

Ben Silliman, Family Life Specialist with the University
of Wyoming's Cooperative Extension Service

[1] flexibility
[2] renewing
[3] lasting a long time
[4] helping to grow or develop

1. Using the context of the sentence, what does *resiliency* mean?

2. Which image describing the strengths of the American family is the most accurate or descriptive for you? Why?

3. What other natural objects/animals/etc. can you compare families to?

B. Quickly skim through the article that follows. Read the first sentence of each paragraph, the headings, and the words that are printed in italics or boldface. Without looking at the text, list some of the main ideas.

C. Now, read the entire passage. As you read it, underline any vocabulary words you do not know. Do not look them up in a dictionary; underline them for now.

The Changing American Family

Cris Beam, *American Baby*

Fewer than 25 percent of American households are made up of a married man and woman with their children. So what do families look like now?

Shifting Demographics

If all you did was watch television commercials for minivans, you might think that the traditional All-American family was still intact—Mom, Dad, dog, and the 2.5 kids buckle up and drive off every day on TV. But ads (depending on your perspective) are either selling aspirations or guilt: This is the family you're supposed to have, supposed to want.

In real life, in big cities and in smaller towns, families are single moms, they're stepfamilies, they're boyfriends and girlfriends not getting married at the moment, they're foster parents, they're two dads or two moms, they're a village. In real life, in 2005, families are richly diverse.

And only getting more so.

In fact, the very definition of "family" is changing dramatically. The year 2000 marked the first time that less than a quarter (23.5 percent) of American households were made up of a married man and woman and one or more of their children—a drop from 45 percent in 1960. This number is expected to fall to 20 percent by 2010.

Why the Changes?

The change in the makeup of the American family is the result of two primary factors, says Martin O'Connell, chief of fertility and family statistics at the U.S. Census Bureau, which collects such figures every 10 years. First, more babies (about a third) are now born out of wedlock, and second, divorce rates continue to climb so that nearly half of all marriage contracts are broken.

What's Normal Now?

The overall attitude toward relationships and commitment has shifted. More than half of female high school seniors say that having a child outside of marriage is acceptable, according to a recent poll from the University of Michigan Survey Research Center. And census data shows that 26 percent of all households are made up of a single person, living alone (as opposed to 13 percent back in 1960).

While a good portion of these singles are likely senior citizens, others are younger career folks who don't feel yesteryear's societal pressure to rush into partnerships. "In 2002, the median age for a woman's first marriage was 27," says O'Connell. That's five years older than it was even in 1980. Sometimes young singles establish their individual identities so solidly that they never marry, even if they have children. These couples may partner up—but without the papers.

Adoption, no marriage: Such was the case with Steve Wilson and Erin Mayes, a couple in their mid-30s living in Austin, Texas. They've been together for 10 years, own a home together, and though they've talked about it, they have decided it isn't necessary to get married. Still, they wanted a family and, last June, adopted a baby boy.

Wedding after baby: Another example is Jared and Lori Goldman, of San Mateo, California. Their relationship was relatively new when Lori got pregnant in 2000. They agreed to raise the child together but didn't get engaged. But not long after their daughter was born, Jared proposed. "Reverse order worked better for us," he says. Lori agrees: "Our wedding felt more meaningful happening on its own time instead of on the traditional schedule. What girl wants a shotgun wedding?"

Single moms on the rise: Of course, because currently one-third of all babies are born out of wedlock, it's no surprise that many mothers remain single. When she got pregnant, Pam Hansell says her boyfriend initially seemed supportive. Then he began dodging her phone calls and e-mails, and eventually cut contact. Deeply hurt but determined to give her child a good life, Hansell moved in with her parents, outside of Philadelphia, and gave birth to a daughter in March. "When I realized I couldn't count on the father, it was devastating. I'm so thankful that family and friends have stepped in," Hansell says.

Two dads: Finally, Dean Larkin and Paul Park are living out another common-in-today's-world scenario. They live together in Los Angeles, and Larkin has a 21-year-old daughter from a previous marriage. Now he and Park are planning a second child, via a surrogate mother. They'd like to marry, but gay marriage is not legal nationally.

Reactions from the Trenches

Perhaps no one has a better ringside seat to all these untraditional family setups than those involved in the childbirth industry. "I've seen unmarried couples come in, lesbian couples, mothers who have been here with one father and then come in with a new father—the family dynamics and structures have changed a lot over the past 25 years," says Barbara Hotelling, president of Lamaze International and a long-time childbirth instructor. Based in Rochester Hills, Michigan, Hotelling probably sees a good cross section of American families and, while she doesn't ask the marital status of her students, estimates that around 20 percent are unmarried, compared with maybe 5 percent when she first began her career. Hotelling has shifted her language with the times. She says she used to call her students moms and dads, but now, "I say 'moms and partners' and hope nobody screams."

Evaluating Credibility of Reading Material

When you are reading additional materials for a course, you should analyze the quality of the information, especially if it comes from a non-academic source. You can ask yourself some questions as you read.

- Who wrote the article? Is the author an expert on the topic (look at the qualifications, job title, etc.)?
- What kind of journal/book/magazine did it appear in?
- Who is quoted in the article? Why did the author choose certain people to quote?
- Is the article biased toward one side of an issue or another?
- When was it written? Is the information current?
- Is the information accurate?

D. Answer these questions about the reading.

1. According to the article, what percentage of American families lives in what are considered traditional nuclear families?

2. What percentage of single households are there now, according to the census data cited in the article?

3. What does the author say are the causes for the changes in family structures?

4. What is considered "normal" when it comes to relationships and commitment, according the majority of high school seniors surveyed and cited in this article?

5. What does this statement mean: *Sometimes young singles establish their individual identities so solidly that they never marry, even if they have children?*

6. Match the person with his or her background/situation. What is the author's purpose for including statements from these people?

Martin O'Connell   Pam Hansell   Dean Larkin and Paul Park

Jared and Lori Goldman   Barbara Hotelling   Steve Wilson and Erin Mayes

a. _____ long-time childbirth instructor

b. _____ unmarried couple who adopted a child

c. _____ chief of fertility and family statistics at the U.S. Census Bureau

d. _____ gay couple who plan to hire a surrogate

e. _____ couple who had children, then married

f. _____ single mother

7. From what magazine/journal does this article come? Does this make a difference in your opinion of the information?

E. Choose some of the words in the passage that you underlined in Activity C. First, write the sentence (or part of the sentence) that contains the vocabulary word. Next, decide which strategy you will use for that vocabulary word from the guidelines in the language box below. If you cannot ignore the word, write the definition in the space provided.

> ### Reviewing Vocabulary Strategies
>
> The following strategies can be used when you are confronted with a vocabulary word you do not know:
>
> 1. Ignore the word.
> 2. Use context clues to help you understand the meaning.
> 3. Guess the meaning from the word's morphology.
> 4. Use a dictionary.
>
> Always begin with number 1. If you can ignore the word, then do so. If the word, however, is necessary to understand the meaning of the sentence, then use one or more of the remaining strategies. Try to become less dependent on your dictionary, as constantly looking up words slows your reading down.

Example:

"... First, more babies (about a third) are now born *out of wedlock,* and second, divorce rates continue to climb so that nearly half of all marriage contracts are broken."

Strategy: 2—use context clues

Definition: outside of marriage (because *wedlock* is related to marriage)

1. _____

_____

Strategy: _____

Definition: _____

2. _____

_____

Strategy: _____

Definition: _____

3. _____

_____

Strategy: _____

Definition: _____

4. _____

_____

Strategy: _____

Definition: _____

5. _____

_____

Strategy: _____

Definition: _____

6. _____

_____

Strategy: _____

Definition: _____

 F. Listen to the introduction of a university radio talk show interview about different work and family roles. For each couple, fill in the first column describing the different work and family situation that each one has. Ignore the rest of the chart right now.

Couples Work/Family Situation	Arguments For	Arguments Against
Scott and Andrea Borden Situation:		
Sabine Price and Stephan Helling Situation:		
Sam and Ann Wurster Situation:		

 G. Listen to the whole interview again, and fill in the chart in Activity F with the arguments for and against the three different work and family situations.

H. In small groups, discuss the arguments that follow. Write statements that refute each argument (show that the argument is incorrect or weak) using your notes from the interview in Activity F and your opinions on the topic.

Argument #1: When both parents work, they spend less time with their children.

Refutation:

Argument #2: It is not really fair for one parent to have to stay home with the children full-time if he or she has an important career.

Refutation:

Argument #3: Most families cannot survive on one salary; it is essential for both parents to work.

Refutation:

Debating Controversial Issues

Debating a topic with an individual or group of people is a good way to practice your speaking skills because it forces you to both organize your thoughts and also "think on your feet." The structure of debates varies greatly. One possible structure follows:

Initial Arguments
- Each team has five to seven minutes to present an initial argument, with the order of team presentations decided by a coin flip.
- Argument should be presented by several members of the group.
- Each team gives two brief succinct "challenge questions" to their opponents at end of argument phase

Team Caucus
- The teams spend five minutes with their members to plan their rebuttal.

Rebuttals
- Each team has five to seven minutes each to respond to the other team's arguments and answer the challenge questions.

Discussion (5–10 minutes)
- The floor is open to the audience for questions and comments.

I. Different topics for debate related to the topic of marriage and family are listed. Your instructor will help you organize into groups for the debates. You do not necessarily have to agree or disagree with a topic; the skills that you will practice are important! Use the guiding questions to help you get organized.

A. Living together before getting married *is/is not* a good test to see if marriage is a good idea.

B. It *is important/not important* to marry someone of the same educational, social, cultural, and racial background as your own.

C. In a family with children, it *is essential/not essential* for the mother to stay home and take care of the children.

D. Marriages between gay and lesbian partners *should/should not* be recognized by the government to receive financial and social benefits.

E. Single women and men *should/should not* be allowed to adopt children.

F. Gay and lesbian couples *should/should not* be allowed to adopt children.

Our Topic: _____

Major arguments in favor of our side:

a. _____
   _____

b. _____
   _____

c. _____
   _____

Challenge questions the other side might ask us:

a. _____
   _____

b. _____
   _____

c. _____
   _____

Challenge questions we want to ask them:

a. _____
   _____

b. _____
   _____

c. _____
   _____

J. Based on one of the debates that you were involved in or listened to, choose one of the topics in Activity I and write a persuasive essay using the organizational pattern information that follows.

Writing a Persuasive Essay

When you write a persuasive essay, you are trying to show the reader that your point of view is the most convincing. You make *assertions*, which are strong statements that show your position/opinion on a topic.

There are many possible organization patterns for persuasive paragraphs and essays. One possible way to organize an essay is to briefly mention the "other" side of the issue in the introduction, but to support your assertions/beliefs strongly in the body paragraphs.

Introductory paragraph
- general background information on topic (mention the "other" side of the issue only to make your thesis statement stronger)
- strong thesis statement with the three best reasons that you have to support your position

Body paragraph #1
- assertion in a topic sentence that relates to your thesis statement (not just a fact—the topic sentence should be a clear and direct assertion of your position)
  —evidence, specific examples, statistics in the paragraph that supports your topic sentence

Body paragraph #2
- assertion in a topic sentence that relates to your thesis statement (not just a fact—the topic sentence should be a clear and direct assertion of your position)
  —evidence, specific examples, statistics in the paragraph that support your topic sentence

Body paragraph #3*
- assertion in a topic sentence that relates to your thesis statement (not just a fact—the topic sentence should be a clear and direct assertion of your position)
  —evidence, specific examples, statistics in the paragraph that support your topic sentence

Conclusion
- restate the topic and your thesis statement (do not introduce any new information in the conclusion)

---

*Some writers believe it is better to put your strongest argument in your final body paragraph.

III. The Older Generation

A. Decide which word logically completes each sentence. Write the letter of the correct answer in the left column.

1. _____ diversity	a. One way to _____ good health is to avoid smoking, eat fruits and vegetables every day, and exercise three or four times a week.
2. _____ rely	b. For _____ reasons, both of my parents had to work when I was growing up to support six children.
3. _____ sufficient	c. The cultural _____ of the United States makes it difficult to talk about "American culture" without making some generalizations.
4. _____ assistance	d. My grandmother lives in a retirement _____ in Florida; the houses are small and there are lot of activities planned for the residents.
5. _____ financial	e. Because of the traffic at rush hour, be sure to give yourself _____ time to get to your first class this morning.
6. _____ factor	f. Young children _____ on their parents to provide them with food, shelter, and clothing.
7. _____ community	g. World leaders met last week in Sweden to discuss ways to provide _____ to less-developed countries.
8. _____ maintain	h. The fact that she spoke about lowering taxes was a key _____ in her re-election for governor of Georgia.

B. Discuss these questions with a partner, making sure you understand the words from Activity A.

1. What kind of community do you want to live in when you are older?

2. Do your grandparents rely on your parents to take care of them?

3. What can people do to maintain good health into our 80s and 90s?

4. What kind of financial assistance do you think the government should provide for the elderly?

5. Name two factors that you think lead to divorce.

6. For a family of four (parents and two children), what size of house do you think is sufficient?

7. What does diversity in family structures refer to?

 C. Listen to the lecture, and take notes on a separate sheet of paper.

> ## Maintaining and Reviewing Notes
> When you take notes in a class, you may not look at them again for several days or weeks. Depending on the type of course and the style of the instructor, you may only have periodic exams on the material, perhaps only a midterm and a final exam. Some suggestions on keeping good notes and learning the material in your notes more effectively and efficiently are:
>
> 1. While you are taking notes, go back and fill in sections when students ask questions or the instructor gives additional examples.
> 2. Compare your notes with a classmate shortly after class.
> 3. Do a periodic cumulative review of your notes throughout the semester so that you are not cramming the night before a major test.

D. Compare your notes with a classmate. Fill in your notes with ideas that you did not write down during the lecture. Answer any questions your classmate has about your notes.

E. Turn in your notes to your instructor. She or he will keep them for several days and ask you questions about the content.

IV. American Homes

 A. With a partner (preferably from a different country than your own), listen to the short description of American homes past and present and fill in the numbers you hear.

The average single family home was _____ square feet in 2004, compared to 1,695 square feet[5] in _____. The size of the kitchen alone has doubled to nearly _____ square feet. Bedrooms are now an average of 12 feet by 12 feet,[6] compared to _____ feet by _____ feet _____ years ago. That's more home for less people. Today's average family size is _____ people. Then, it was _____ people.

Have you been invited to an American's home for dinner, a party, a backyard barbecue, etc.? Throughout this book, we have talked about cultural values and how these values affect behavior. In small groups, discuss these questions.

1. Look at the floor plan of a modern, typical American home on page 149. Compare this with typical homes in your culture. What are the similarities and differences?

2. How are bathrooms in American homes different from those in homes in your culture? Are the doors to bathrooms usually kept open or closed when not in use?

3. Do you think children should get their own rooms? Why or why not?

4. Do you have pets? If so, do they sleep/eat inside the house? Do they sleep on the bed with you?

---

[5] 516.6 square meters
[6] 3.66 square meters

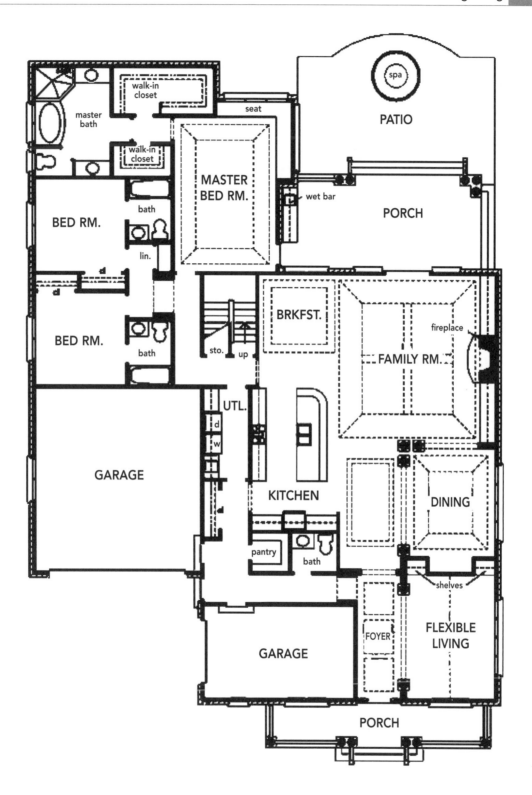

V. Values Application

A. Each statement describes an aspect of American families. Choose the American value(s) each one represents among the values discussed in Chapter 1.

Statement	Value(s)
1. A boy and his two sisters each have their own room.	
2. A 13-year-old daughter is the only vegetarian in the family, so she cooks a different meal from her family's almost every night.	
3. Both the mother and father of a family of five work, but they take turns cooking and cleaning.	
4. Each family member has certain jobs around the house to take care of every week.	
5. A grandfather moved into a retirement home after his wife died, even though his two sons live in the same city as he does.	
6. A 14-year-old child is given the choice to live with either his recently divorced mother or father.	
7. As the guests arrive for a dinner party, each one is given a tour of the house and the backyard.	
8. Some women choose not to take their husband's last name when they marry.	

Appendix

Vocabulary from the Academic Word List Appearing in This Text

Chapter 1
affect
analyze
aspect
assume
comma
communication
communities
complex
comprise
concentrate
conflicts
context
contribute
cooperation
created
culture
dash
data
distinctive
diversity
dominate
economic
emphasize
establish
ethnic
evaluate
evolve
expensive
factor
focus

founded
goal
image
individualism
institution
involved
job
major
nevertheless
occurred
participant
period
physical
policy
psychology
research
resource
reveal
revolution
role
similar
text
tradition
transform

Chapter 2
aware
communicate
conduct
constant
consultant

culture
encounter
environment
expert
feature
financial
focus
image
inappropriate
income
indicator
integrity
interaction
interpret
item
obviously
occupation
period
physical
professional
psychologist
relax
reveal
significant
topic

Chapter 3
adult
aid
annual
approximate

cite
colleague
consumed
contributed
diverse
economy
equipment
final
income
institute
intelligence
job
journal
maintain
majority
medical
minor
participant
percent
physical
professionally
promote
require
research
revenue
series
similar
source
status
stress
struck out

team
trend
unique

Chapter 4
academic
administration
approximately
attain
community
contrast
coordination
drafting
economics
environment
fees
funded
goal
grant
institution
interact
involved
job
obtain
occupational
period
physical
preliminary
prior
range
required
research
resident
specifically
structure
technical
variation

Chapter 5
achievement
annual
area
assembly
authority
available
benefits
category
commission
communicate
compiled
conclusion
consume
cooperating
corporate
creative
culture
design
detect
dimension
enable
environment
equipment
evaluate
factor
finally
globally
implement
individualism
intense
involved
item
job
labels
labor
likewise
majority

manual
medical
medium
mentality
notion
obvious
percentage
period
plus
processes
professional
projects
promote
range
require
research
sector
shift
specific
styling
task
team
technical
technology
traditional
transformation
vary

Chapter 6
assistance
attitude
commitment
community
contact
contract
couple
data
definition

diversity
dramatically
dynamics
establish
estimate
eventually
factors
finally
financial
identities
individual
initially
instructor
involved
legal
maintain
normal
overall
partnership
percent
perspective
portion
previous
primary
reaction
rely
research
reverse
scenario
schedule
shift
statistics
structure
sufficient
survey
traditional
via